Office of National Marine Sanctuaries
National Oceanic and Atmospheric Administration

NATIONAL MARINE
SANCTUARIES

Thunder Bay
National Marine Sanctuary

CONDITION
REPORT 2013

February 2013

U.S. Department of Commerce
Rebecca Blank, Acting Secretary

National Oceanic and Atmospheric Administration
Jane Lubchenco, Ph.D.,
Under Secretary of Commerce for Oceans and Atmosphere

National Ocean Service
Holly Bamford, Ph.D., Assistant Administrator

Office of National Marine Sanctuaries
Daniel J. Basta, Director

National Oceanic and Atmospheric Administration
Office of National Marine Sanctuaries
1305 East-West Highway
Silver Spring, MD 20910
301-713-3125
http://sanctuaries.noaa.gov

Thunder Bay National Marine Sanctuary
500 W. Fletcher Street
Alpena, MI 49707
989-356-8805
http://www.thunderbay.noaa.gov

Report Authors:

Thunder Bay National Marine Sanctuary:
Russ Green

Office of National Marine Sanctuaries
Kathy Broughton, Stephen R. Gittings

Copy Editor: Matt Dozier

Layout: Matt McIntosh

Suggested Citation:

Office of National Marine Sanctuaries. 2013. Thunder Bay National Marine Sanctuary Condition Report 2013. U.S. Department of Commerce, National Oceanic and Atmospheric Administration, Office of National Marine Sanctuaries, Silver Spring, MD. 80 pp.

NATIONAL MARINE
SANCTUARIES

Table of Contents

Thunder Bay National Marine Sanctuary

- *Thunder Bay National Marine Sanctuary was designated on Oct. 7, 2000, to protect a nationally significant collection of shipwrecks and other maritime heritage resources.*

- *The sanctuary is located in northwestern Lake Huron off Alpena, Mich., and is jointly managed by NOAA and the state of Michigan.*

- *The 448-square-mile sanctuary protects one of America's best-preserved collections of historic shipwrecks.*

- *Historical research indicates that as many as 200 shipwrecks lie in and around Thunder Bay, representing a century and a half of maritime commerce and travel on the Great Lakes. To date, 45 shipwrecks have been discovered in the sanctuary, and an additional 47 have been located outside sanctuary boundaries in an area currently being considered for sanctuary expansion.*

- *It is the first sanctuary to focus solely on a large collection of maritime heritage resources, and the only sanctuary in the Great Lakes.*

About this Report

This "condition report" provides a summary of resources in the Thunder Bay National Marine Sanctuary (sanctuary)[1], pressures on those resources, current conditions and trends, and management responses to the pressures that threaten the integrity of sanctuary resources. Specifically, the document includes information on the status and trends of water quality, habitat, living resources and maritime archaeological resources, and the human activities that affect them. It presents responses to a set of questions posed to all sanctuaries (Appendix A). Resource status of Thunder Bay is rated on a scale from good to poor, and the timelines used for comparison vary from topic to topic. Trends in the status of resources are also reported, and are generally based on observed changes in status over the past five years, unless otherwise specified.

Sanctuary staff consulted with a group of outside experts familiar with the resources and with knowledge of previous and current scientific investigations in the sanctuary. Evaluations of status and trends are based on interpretation of quantitative and, when necessary, non-quantitative assessments, and the observations of scientists, managers and users. The ratings reflect the collective interpretation of the status of local issues of concern among sanctuary program staff and outside experts based on their knowledge and perception of local problems. The final ratings were determined by sanctuary staff. This report has been peer reviewed and complies with the White House Office of Management and Budget's peer review standards as outlined in the Final Information Quality Bulletin for Peer Review.

This is the first attempt to describe comprehensively the status, pressures and trends of resources at Thunder Bay National Marine Sanctuary. Additionally, the report helps identify gaps in current monitoring efforts, as well as causal factors that may require monitoring and potential remediation in the years to come. The data discussed will enable the sanctuary to not only acknowledge prior changes in resource status, but will provide guidance for future management challenges.

Summary and Findings

Designated in 2000, Thunder Bay National Marine Sanctuary protects a nationally significant collection of historic shipwrecks and related maritime cultural resources in northern Lake Huron. Through research, resource protection and education, the sanctuary works to ensure that these important historic, archaeological and recreational sites are preserved for current and future generations. The variety of shipwreck types, genres, depths and locations combined with their excellent states of preservation make the area in and around the sanctuary a haven for divers, kayakers and snorkelers, as well as historians, archaeologists and students of all ages. The sanctuary's Great Lakes Maritime Heritage Center helps connect non-divers with these treasures, while also serving as a base of operations for many researchers and expeditions each year. Additionally, the sanctuary serves as an anchor for heritage tourism, helping to attract businesses that have a positive impact on the local economy, and also supports a wide range of multidisciplinary research. Strong regional interest in the sanctuary by the public, local and state government, and non-government organizations has prompted the sanctuary's advisory council to recommend expanding the sanctuary boundaries, a process that is currently underway and summarized

---

[1]Thunder Bay National Marine Sanctuary is jointly managed by the National Oceanic and Atmospheric Administra ion and the state of Michigan.

in this report. Consequently, there are many stakeholders with an interest in the sanctuary and the condition of its resources.

Overall, the condition of the sanctuary's maritime archaeological resources, both individually and as a collection, is considered to be good. Management actions such as the sanctuary's mooring buoy program, avocational archaeological training for divers, and targeted education and outreach programs are helping to limit human impacts on sanctuary resources. While some human impacts on sanctuary resources have been mitigated via strategic management actions and education programs, other pressures, such as impacts from non-indigenous species (e.g., zebra mussels), are more difficult to control. Increased sanctuary-driven research is producing a better understanding of the state of sanctuary resources and the pressures on them, as well as establishing a baseline for future monitoring, while at the same time allowing for enhanced education and outreach products. Likewise, sanctuary partners, including volunteer divers, are currently conducting research — both archaeological and multidisciplinary — at the highest levels since the sanctuary's designation. Law enforcement continues to be an area of concern for the sanctuary, though the U.S. Coast Guard Alpena Station and Michigan DNR conduct on-water patrols aimed at resource protection.

It should be noted that this condition report reflects Thunder Bay National Marine Sanctuary's management focus on maritime archaeological resources, chiefly historic shipwrecks, but also related heritage resources such as submerged docks, piers and other elements of maritime infrastructure.[2] Consequently, this condition report does not directly address other aspects of the ecosystem (e.g., habitat and living resource quality). Exceptions, however, occur when there is a causal relationship between maritime archaeological resources and the ecosystem (e.g., the colonization of shipwrecks by non-indigenous mussels). Water quality issues are addressed in this report, but only where a nexus between shipwrecks and water quality could be identified (e.g., chiefly where poor water quality might prohibit public visitation of sanctuary resources). In general, water quality in the sanctuary as it relates to public access to maritime archaeological resources is considered to be good/fair. For the most part, changing or poor water quality is not an issue in Thunder Bay, nor is the resultant potential for decreased public visitation.

National Marine Sanctuary System and System-Wide Monitoring

The National Marine Sanctuary System manages marine areas in both nearshore and open ocean waters that range in size from less than one to almost 140,000 square miles (362,598 square kilometers). Each area has its own concerns and requirements for environmental monitoring, but ecosystem structure and function in all these areas have similarities and are influenced by common factors that interact in comparable ways. Furthermore, the human influences that affect the structure and function of these sites are similar in a number of ways. For these reasons, in 2001 the program began to implement System-Wide Monitoring (SWiM). The monitoring framework (NMSP 2004) facilitates the development of effective, ecosystem-based monitoring programs that address management information needs using a design process that can be applied in a consistent way at multiple spatial scales and to multiple resource types. It identifies four primary components common among marine ecosystems: water, habitats, living resources and maritime archaeological resources.

By assuming that a common marine ecosystem framework can be applied to all places, the National Marine Sanctuary System developed a series of questions that are posed to every sanctuary and used as evaluation criteria to assess resource condition and trends. The questions, which are shown on the following page and explained in Appendix A, are derived from both a generalized ecosystem framework and from the National Marine Sanctuary System's mission. They are widely applicable across the system of areas managed by the sanctuary program and provide a tool with which the program can measure its progress toward maintaining and improving resource quality throughout the system.

Similar reports summarizing resource status and trends will be prepared for each marine sanctuary approximately every five years and updated as new information allows. The information in this report is intended to help set the stage for the management plan review process. The report also helps sanctuary staff identify monitoring, characterization and research priorities to address gaps, day-to-day information needs and new threats.

---

[2]The potential for submerged prehistoric sites also exists wi hin he sanctuary and region (see *Response* sec ion).

Thunder Bay National Marine Sanctuary Condition Summary Table

The following table summarizes the "State of Sanctuary Resources" section of this report. The first two columns list 17 questions used to rate the condition and trends for qualities of water, habitat, living resources and maritime archaeological resources. The Rating column consists of a color, indicating resource condition, and a symbol, indicating trend (see key for definitions). The Basis for Judgment column provides a short statement or list of criteria used to justify the rating. The Description of Findings column presents the statement that best characterizes resource status, and corresponds to the assigned color rating. The Description of Findings statements are customized for all possible ratings for each question. Please see Appendix A for further clarification of the questions and the Description of Findings statements. The Response column describes current or proposed management responses to pressures impacting sanctuary resources.

This condition report reflects Thunder Bay National Marine Sanctuary's management focus on maritime archaeological resources, chiefly historic shipwrecks. Consequently, this condition report does not directly address other aspects of the ecosystem (e.g., habitat and living resource quality). Exceptions, however, occur when there is a causal relationship between maritime archaeological resources and the ecosystem (e.g., the colonization of shipwrecks by non-indigenous mussels). It should also be noted that although the sanctuary does not manage non-archaeological resources, it does encourage, facilitate and participate in a wide range of multidisciplinary research, monitoring and data acquisition efforts (see *Response* section).

Status: | Good | Good/Fair | Fair | Fair/Poor | Poor | Undet. |

Trends:
Conditions appear to be improving .... ▲
Conditions do not appear to be changing .... —
Conditions appear to be declining .... ▼
Undetermined trend .... ?
Question not applicable .... N/A

#	Questions/Resources	Rating	Basis for Judgment	Description of Findings	Sanctuary Response
WATER					
1	Are specific or multiple stressors, including changing oceanographic and atmospheric conditions, affecting water quality and how are they changing?	?	Invasive zebra and quagga mussels have altered water quality; ice coverage has declined and water levels have fluctuated. Changes in water quality could negatively impact public access to sanctuary resources.	Selected conditions may degrade maritime archaeological resources, but are not likely to cause substantial or persistent declines.	Although the sanctuary exclusively manages maritime archaeological resources, it supports and facilitates multidisciplinary research aimed at better understanding the natural resources of Thunder Bay and Lake Huron. Some of these efforts may lead to a better understanding of water quality in and around the sanctuary.
2	What is the eutrophic condition of sanctuary waters and how is it changing?	—	Algal blooms that lead to beach closures and reduced water quality could negatively impact the public's access to sanctuary resources.	Selected conditions may cause measurable but not severe declines in maritime archaeological resources.	
3	Do sanctuary waters pose risks to human health and how are they changing?	—	Documented swimming advisories and beach closures may limit the public's access to sanctuary resources.	Selected conditions that have the potential to affect human health may exist, but human impacts have not been reported.	
4	What are the levels of human activities that may influence water quality and how are they changing?	▲	Few point sources, however, nonpoint sources can occur after heavy rain. Poor water quality could limit the public's access to sanctuary resources.	Some potentially harmful activities exist, but they do not appear to have had a negative effect on water quality.	

Table is continued on the following page.

Thunder Bay National Marine Sanctuary Condition Summary Table (Continued)

#	Questions/Resources	Rating	Basis for Judgment	Description of Findings	Sanctuary Response
HABITAT					
5	What is the abundance and distribution of major habitat types and how is it changing?	N/A	Thunder Bay National Marine Sanctuary regulations specify the management of maritime archaeological resources. For this reason, Questions 5 - 8 were deemed "not applicable."	N/A	Although the sanctuary exclusively manages maritime archaeological resources, it supports and facilitates multidisciplinary research aimed at better understanding the natural resources of Thunder Bay and Lake Huron. Some of these efforts may lead to a better understanding of habitat quality in and around the sanctuary.
6	What is the condition of biologically structured habitats and how is it changing?	N/A		N/A	
7	What are the contaminant concentrations in sanctuary habitats and how are they changing?	N/A		N/A	
8	What are the levels of human activities that may influence habitat quality and how are they changing?	N/A		N/A	
LIVING RESOURCES					
9	What is the status of biodiversity and how is it changing?	N/A	Thunder Bay National Marine Sanctuary regulations specify the management of maritime archaeological resources. For this reason, Questions 9 & 10 were deemed "not applicable."	N/A	Although the sanctuary only manages maritime archaeological resources, it supports and facilitates multidisciplinary research aimed at better understanding the natural resources of Thunder Bay and Lake Huron. Some of these efforts may lead to a better understanding of living resources (particularly invasive mussels) in and around the sanctuary.
10	What is the status of environmentally sustainable fishing and how is it changing?	N/A		N/A	
11	What is the status of non-indigenous species and how is it changing?	—	Zebra and quagga mussel colonization is causing archaeological resources to deteriorate and hinders the ability to accurately and precisely conduct archaeological documentation.	Non-indigenous species have caused or are likely to cause severe declines in maritime archaeological resources.	
12	What is the status of key species and how is it changing?	N/A	Thunder Bay National Marine Sanctuary regulations specify the management of maritime archaeological resources. For this reason, Questions 12 & 13 were deemed "not applicable."	N/A	
13	What is the condition or health of key species and how is it changing?	N/A		N/A	
14	What are the levels of human activities that may influence living resource quality and how are they changing?	—	The original vector for invasion is not likely to affect the future of existing mussels, but could introduce other non-indigenous species.	Some potentially harmful activities exist, but they do not appear to have had a negative effect on maritime archaeological resources.	
MARITIME ARCHAEOLOGICAL RESOURCES					
15	What is the integrity of known maritime archaeological resources and how is it changing?	▼	Mussel colonization and natural deterioration will persist, but resulting declines in integrity are slow. Management actions have slowed diver and boating impacts.	Selected archaeological resources exhibit indications of disturbance, but there appears to have been little or no reduction in historical, scientific or educational value.	The sanctuary assesses and documents maritime archaeological resources to establish each site's current state of preservation and to create a baseline for monitoring future impacts. The sanctuary maintains a growing number of moorings at sanctuary shipwrecks, and conducts effective education and outreach programs aimed at fostering a greater preservation ethic among divers and the public.
16	Do known maritime archaeological resources pose an environmental hazard and how is this threat changing?	—	Few, if any, wrecks pose an environmental threat, and those that do are localized.	Known maritime archaeological resources pose few or no environmental threats.	
17	What are the levels of human activities that may influence maritime archaeological resource quality and how are they changing?	▲	All human activities that pose a threat to maritime archaeological resources are on the decline due to management actions (e.g., mooring, education, and enforcement activities).	Selected activities have resulted in measurable impacts to maritime archaeological resources, but evidence suggests effects are localized, not widespread.	

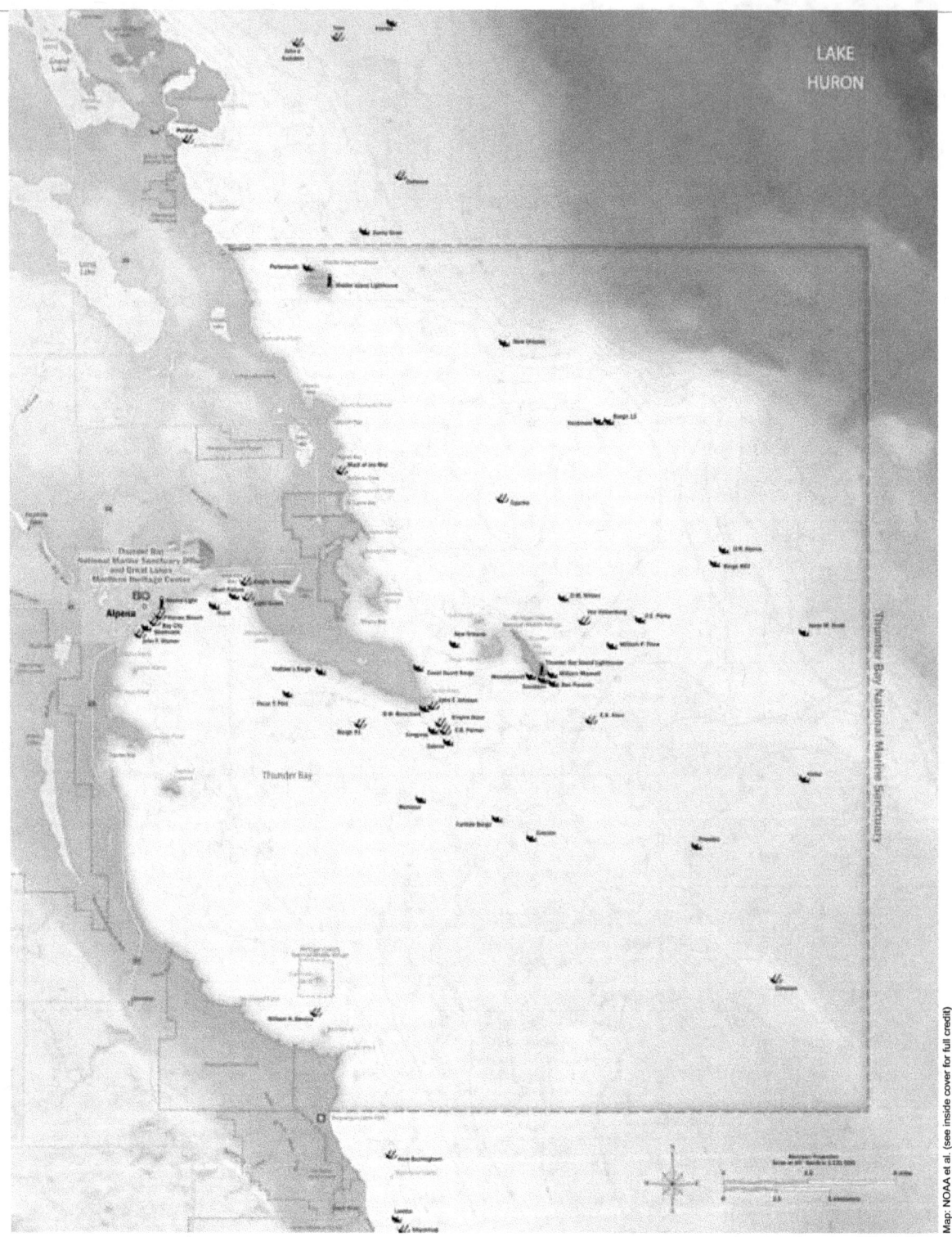

Located in northwestern Lake Huron, the 448-square-mile Thunder Bay National Marine Sanctuary protects one of America's best-preserved and nationally-significant collections of shipwrecks. Fire, ice, collisions, and storms have claimed over 200 vessels in and around Thunder Bay. To date, 45 shipwrecks have been discovered within the sanctuary and an additional 47 wrecks have been located outside of the sanctuary boundaries.

Map: NOAA et al. (see inside cover for full credit)

Site History and Resources

For more than 12,000 years, people have traveled on the Great Lakes. From Native American dugout canoes to wooden sailing craft and steel freighters, thousands of ships have made millions of voyages across the Inland Seas. The last 150 years have been particularly explosive, transforming the region into one of the world's busiest waterways. However, with extraordinary growth comes adversity. Fire, ice, collisions and storms have claimed nearly 200 vessels in and around Thunder Bay, including pioneer steamboats, majestic wooden schooners and huge steel freighters. Today, the 448-square-mile Thunder Bay National Marine Sanctuary protects one of America's best-preserved and nationally significant collections of shipwrecks. These important archaeological and recreational sites capture dramatic moments from centuries that transformed America. As a collection, they illuminate an era of enormous national growth and remind us of risks taken and tragedies endured.

Currently, 45 known shipwrecks are located in the sanctuary, with an additional 47 sites in an area currently being considered for sanctuary expansion (see *Response* section). The historical record suggests that as many as 100 shipwrecks are yet to be found in this northern region of Lake Huron. Although the sheer number of shipwrecks in and around the sanctuary is substantial, it is the wide range of vessel types and associated time span that imparts much of the collection's national significance. From an 1844 side-wheel steamer carrying passengers during America's westward expansion to a modern 500-foot German freighter laden with steel for the auto industry, the shipwrecks of Thunder Bay represent a microcosm of maritime commerce and travel on the Great Lakes.

Remarkable preservation equally contributes to the collection's national significance. Lake Huron's cold, fresh water ensures that the Thunder Bay region's shipwrecks are among the best preserved in the world (Figures 1 and 2). Many sites have remained virtually unchanged for over 150 years. With masts still standing, deck hardware in place and many artifacts often surviving, sites located in deeper waters are true time capsules. Other shipwrecks lay broken up but well-preserved in shallower waters. Readily accessible by kayakers, snorkelers and divers of all abilities, these sites often provide sanctuary users with their first shipwreck experience. Believing that people will protect what they value, the sanctuary has made encouraging and facilitating public access to its historic shipwrecks a cornerstone of its resource protection efforts. Deep or shallow, intact or broken up, all of the sanctuary's shipwrecks possess historical, archaeological and recreational value.

The final contributing element to the sanctuary's national significance is its proven ability to creatively present the collection and its

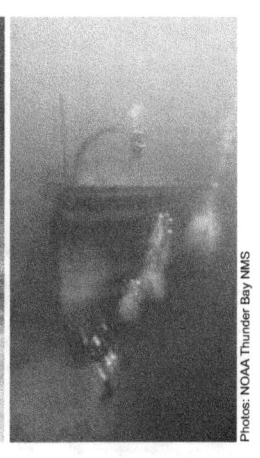

Photos: NOAA Thunder Bay NMS

Figures 1 and 2. Deep or shallow, Lake Huron's cold, fresh water keeps shipwrecks well-preserved. Left: Resting in 15 feet of water, the wreck of the steamer *Monohansett* is a popular destination for kayaking and snorkeling, and in 2011 became the centerpiece of a new glass bottom boat tour operating out of Alpena. Right: The bow of the steamer *Florida* rests in 200 feet of water outside the sanctuary's northern boundary. Incredibly well-preserved, sites like this offer a one-of-a-kind opportunity for historians, archaeologists and experienced technical divers.

significance to the American people. As with providing physical access to shipwrecks, the sanctuary's education and outreach efforts provide access to those resources for non-divers, while fostering an awareness and appreciation for the Great Lakes and their history. Thunder Bay National Marine Sanctuary protects our rich national maritime heritage through education, research and resource protection.

Location

The 448-square-mile Thunder Bay National Marine Sanctuary is located in northwestern Lake Huron (Figure 3). The sanctuary's northern and southern boundaries are defined by the lakeward extension of the respective Alpena County borders, while its eastern boundary is 83 degrees west longitude, approximately 20 miles from Alpena. The sanctuary's western boundary follows the contours of the Michigan shoreline at the ordinary high-water mark. Forty-five known shipwrecks are found in this area.

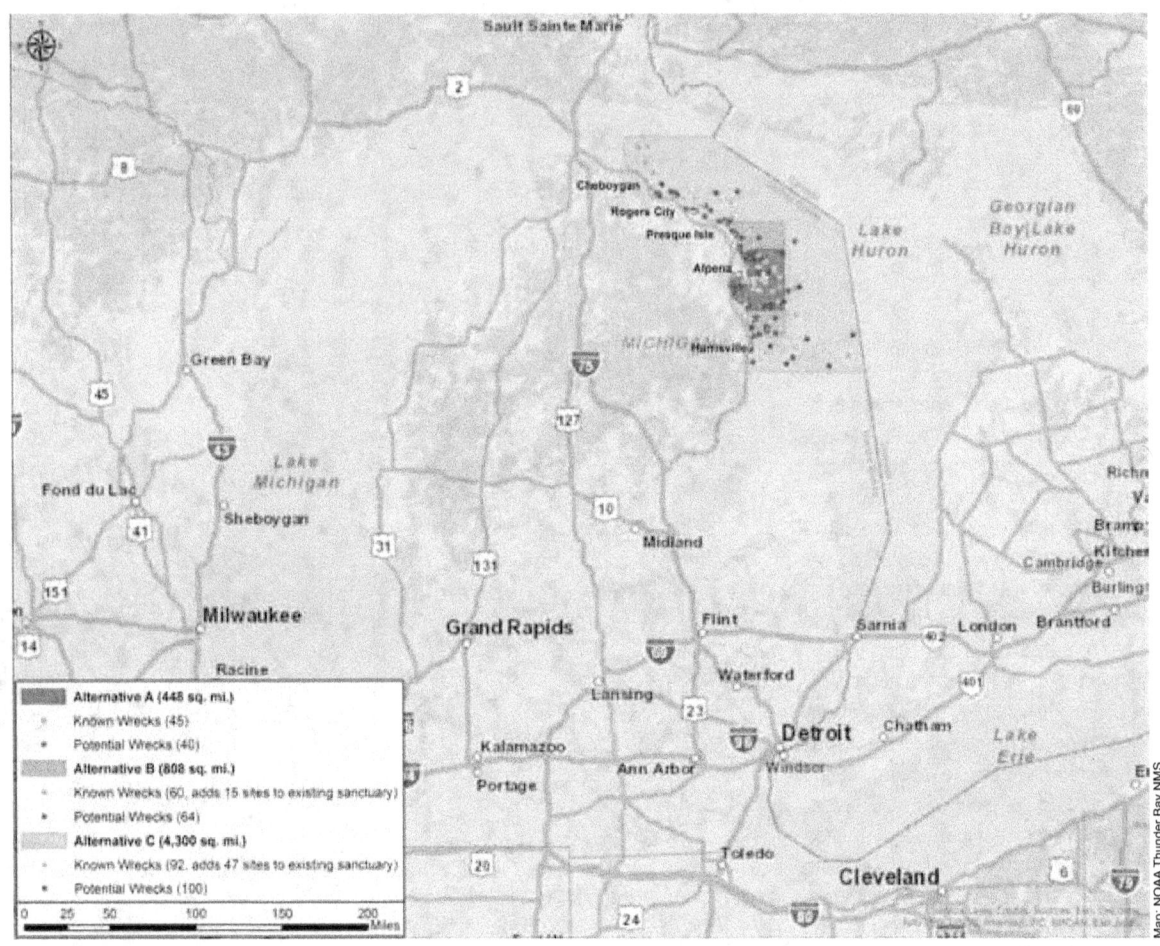

Figure 3. Thunder Bay National Marine Sanctuary is located in northwestern Lake Huron. Currently, 45 known shipwrecks are located within the 448-square-mile sanctuary, indicated by the dark blue area. Based on a recommendation by the sanctuary's advisory council and other public input, NOAA is currently engaged in a process to examine boundary expansion. NOAA's preferred expansion area would add 47 known shipwrecks to the sanctuary. The area is shown in light blue; see also *Response* section.

The sanctuary's 2000 designation documents called on the sanctuary to evaluate an expansion of its boundaries within five years of designation. In 2007, the Thunder Bay Sanctuary Advisory Council, as part of the sanctuary's management plan process, recommended that the sanctuary expand its boundaries to protect shipwrecks and other maritime archaeological resources in waters off the two counties adjacent to Alpena County (Alcona and Presque Isle counties). Based on this and other public input, the sanctuary's Final Management Plan (TBNMS 2009) includes a strategy calling on the sanctuary to evaluate this boundary alternative. Consequently, NOAA is currently engaged in an administrative process to expand the sanctuary's boundaries (see *Response* section), based on the Sanctuary Advisory Council's recommended study area. Expansion would increase the sanctuary boundary to 4,300-square-miles. This would add 47 shipwrecks to the sanctuary. The new boundary would include all 92 historic shipwrecks in Alpena, Alcona and Presque Isle counties, and five shipwrecks from Mackinaw and Cheboygan counties (Figure 3).

Because of the many historically, archaeologically and recreationally significant shipwrecks outside the sanctuary's current boundaries, NOAA and the state of Michigan have increasingly included these sites in their research and resource protection efforts. The state of these resources, as well as the pressures on them and the sanctuary's response to these pressures, are included in this report.

Designation and Management

In 1981, the state of Michigan created the Thunder Bay Underwater Preserve, a 290-square-mile area designated as the first of 11 preserves authorized by Michigan's "Bottomlands Act.[3]" On Oct. 7, 2000 the Secretary of Commerce, under the National Marine Sanctuaries Act, designated the 448-sqaure-mile Thunder Bay National Marine Sanctuary and Underwater Preserve as the nation's 13th national marine sanctuary (Michigan's "Bottomlands Act" was also amended so that the state preserve boundaries matched those of the sanctuary).

The 448-square-mile area of northwestern Lake Huron is now both a national marine sanctuary and a state underwater preserve. The sanctuary is managed jointly by the National Oceanic and Atmospheric Administration (NOAA) and the state of Michigan. The sanctuary superintendent manages the day-to-day operations and activities of the site, while a Joint Management Committee, consisting of the director of the Office of National Marine Sanctuaries and the director of the Michigan Historical Center, makes major policy, budget and management decisions. In addition, an advisory council provides advice to the sanctuary superintendent. Members of the advisory council represent the community's interests, including government, education, maritime history and interpretation, fishing, diving, tourism, economic development, the state-designated underwater preserve, and the community at large.

The Michigan Historical Center

The Michigan Historical Center represents the state of Michigan in managing the Thunder Bay National Marine Sanctuary. The center comprises the Michigan Historical Museum System and the Archives of Michigan. The center builds programs and alliances that preserve and interpret Michigan's past and help people discover, enjoy, and find inspiration in their heritage. The center is part of the Michigan Department of Natural Resources (DNR). The DNR is committed to the conservation, protection, management, use and enjoyment of the state's natural and cultural resources for current and future generations.

Sanctuary Historical Context

From historical and archaeological perspectives, the resources of Thunder Bay National Marine Sanctuary represent a window into both America's past and the local and regional history of the area. The area's national significance — the basis for its designation as a national marine sanctuary — in many ways runs parallel with local history; the histories are connected, complementary and inform each other. This section briefly describes the sanctuary's broader historical context.

The Great Lakes and their connecting waterways provide a natural highway extending over a thousand miles into the heart of North America. For centuries before European contact, these inland seas and tributaries served as important lines of trade and communication for Native Americans. Over the past 300 years, these waters have been further exploited by Euro-Americans and have greatly contributed to the growth of the North American interior. Marine transport on the Great Lakes played a crucial role in the exploration, settlement and industrialization of the region.

During the 19th and early 20th centuries, the Great Lakes of North America evolved from an isolated maritime frontier on the western edge of the Atlantic World into the nation's busiest and the world's most significant industrial waterway, where innovative ships and technologies moved raw materials and agricultural products in larger quantities and at lower costs than at any previous time in history. During this period, entrepreneurs and shipbuilders on the Great Lakes launched tens of thousands of ships of many different designs. Sailing schooners, grand palace steamers, revolutionary propeller-driven passenger ships and industrial bulk carriers transported America's business and industry. In the process, they brought hundreds of thousands of people to the Midwest and made possible the dramatic growth of the region's farms, cities and industries. The Midwest, and indeed the American nation, could not have developed with such speed and with such vast economic and social consequences without the Great Lakes.

Dubbed "Shipwreck Alley," the treacherous waters around Thunder Bay have claimed nearly 200 ships. Intense weather patterns, islands and rocky shoals, heavy vessel traffic and converging shipping lanes all contributed to the area's vast collection of shipwrecks. These submerged archaeological sites are nearly a complete collection of Great Lakes vessel types, from small schooners and pioneer steamboats of the 1830s to enormous industrial bulk carriers that supported the Midwest's heavy industries during the 20th century. Among the wrecks in and around the sanctuary are those vessels

[3]Bottomlands Act, 1980 PA 184, MCL 299.51 et seq. The state's preserve program is presen ly authorized by Part 761 of the Natural Resources and Environmental Protec ion Act, 1994 PA 451

[4]The official name of the sanctuary is the Thunder Bay National Marine Sanctuary and Underwater Preserve. To simplify the name, the Joint Management Committee has agreed to use the name Thunder Bay National Marine Sanctuary.

Figures 4 and 5. Left: The scattered remains of the paddle wheel steamer *New Orleans* (1843-1849; 13-foot depth) are a complex artifact. Wrecked in Thunder Bay in 1849, the 185-foot side-wheel steamer carried thousands of passengers from Buffalo to the western Great Lakes during its career. Today, the shallow site is an excellent venue for diving, snorkeling, kayaking and glass bottom boat excursions. Right: The paddle wheel steamer *Marine City* (1866-1880; five-foot depth) carried passengers and freight on a regular schedule to Alpena and other port towns along Lake Huron. The vessel sank in 1880 with the loss of 20 lives.

that carried immigrants and pioneers traveling west for new homes, schooners carrying Midwestern grain and lumber, passengers and package freight steamers, and evolving generations of bulk freighters specially designed to carry iron ore, coal, grain, cement and other bulk commodities. They are evidence of the Great Lakes' pervasive influence in regional and national history, and they capture the cultural, personal, environmental, technological and economic aspects of maritime history. Finally, the shipwrecks identified in this report reflect the movement, bravery, tenacity and innovative spirit of generations of maritime people.

Maritime Archaeological Resources

The following narrative offers a representative account of maritime archaeological resources, chiefly historic shipwrecks, both in the current sanctuary boundaries and in the larger area being considered for sanctuary expansion.[5] They are arranged here by vessel type and significance. After the name of each shipwreck, in parentheses, are the dates it was built and lost, as well as the depth of water that the site is located in. A complete list of known shipwrecks can be found in Appendix C.

Early Steam

The oldest known shipwreck in Thunder Bay is the wooden paddle wheel steamer *New Orleans* (Figure 4). Rebuilt in 1843 on the hull of the burned steamer *Vermillion*, *New Orleans* ran aground west of Sugar Island on June 15, 1849, and now rests in 13 feet of water. Fishermen from Thunder Bay Island and Sugar Island rescued the passengers and crew,

and salvagers later recovered most of the cargo and machinery. Early steam paddle wheelers such as *New Orleans* are prime examples of the transition from sail to steam. Most were designed to carry large cargoes in their holds, while the upper works were elaborately decorated and furnished to accommodate ticketed passengers, many of them heading west to settle on the American frontier. In addition to *New Orleans*, two other paddle wheelers, *Benjamin Franklin* (1842-1850; 15-foot depth) and *Albany* (1846-1853; five-foot depth), grounded at Thunder Bay Island and Presque Isle, respectively. All three were extensively salvaged. The lower bilge, hull fragments, stern post and boiler area remnants of the *New Orleans* make for a complex and interesting shallow wreck site to visit. Little remains of the *Albany* and *Franklin* except the lower hull structure of each vessel, though *Franklin's* shafts, boilers and machinery remain on the lake bottom only a few hundred yards from the Thunder Bay Island lighthouse. The side-wheel steamer *Marine City* (1866-1880; five-foot depth) is similarly broken up in shallow water north of the Sturgeon Point Lighthouse (Figure 5). Carrying more than 150 people, the wooden vessel burned and sank in 1880 with the tragic loss of 20 lives.

Schooners

Several dozen wooden schooners are located in and around the sanctuary. The quintessential workhorse of the day, schooners sailed the lakes by the thousands in the late 19th century, and dozens were lost around Thunder Bay. Many schooners such as *E.B. Allen* (Figure 6, 1864-1871; 100-foot depth), *Lucinda Van Valkenburg* (1862-1887; 60-foot depth), *Cornelia B. Windiate* (1874-1875; 180-foot depth), *Kyle Spangler* (1856-1860; 180-foot depth), *F.T. Barney* (1856-1868; 160-

[5] Much of this sec ion is excerpted from Lusardi 2011.

 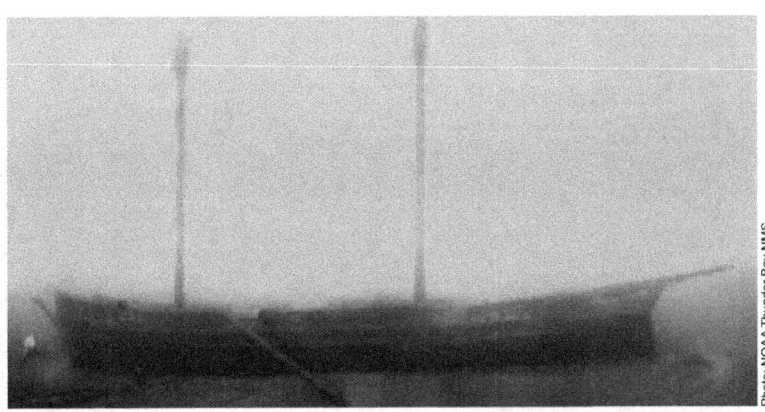

Photo: NOAA Thunder Bay NMS

Photo: NOAA Thunder Bay NMS

Figure 6. Left: The schooner *E. B. Allen* rests in 100 feet of water and displays a degree of preservation typical in this depth range. Heavy traffic, compounded by darkness or fog, often made for a deadly combination near Thunder Bay. In 1868, the *E. B. Allen* collided off Presque Isle with the schooner *Persian*, sending the *Persian* to the bottom and drowning all on board. Three years later, the *E. B. Allen* met a similar fate off Thunder Bay after colliding with the sailing vessel *Newsboy*. Carrying a full cargo of Wisconsin wheat, the *E. B. Allen* sank quickly. Marked with a permanent sanctuary mooring, this canal-sized schooner is a popular dive site.

Figure 7. Right: A photomosaic of the schooner *Defiance*, resting in 185 feet of water outside the sanctuary's northern boundary. Many popular, intact shipwrecks lay in deeper waters outside the sanctuary. In an effort to better understand and protect these impressive time capsules, sanctuary archaeologists regularly work outside sanctuary boundaries.

foot depth), and *Typo* (1873-1899; 160-foot depth), have become very popular recreational and technical dive destinations. Discovered by the sanctuary in 2011, the schooner *M.F. Merrick* (1863-1889; 300-foot depth), lost with four crew after a collision with a southbound steamer, is the latest addition to this list. These shipwrecks represent a type of vessel typical of the late 19th century known as a canaler, designed with dimensions specifically to allow passage through the Welland Canal connecting Lakes Erie and Ontario. The hulls configured as nearly as possible to the locks' dimensions (150 feet by 26 feet), and even the bowsprits were hinged to allow maximum hull length, and thus, cargo carrying capacity. By 1871, 2,000 canalers plied the Great Lakes, most carrying grain eastward and coal westward. All of the aforementioned schooners, with the exception of *Windiate*, were sunk as result of a collision with other vessels in the busy shipping lanes off Alpena and Presque Isle. With no survivors or witnesses, *Windiate's* sinking remains a mystery, although unpredictable November weather was likely a factor. Designed to carry 16,000 bushels of wheat, but reportedly carrying 19,000, she may also have been dangerously overloaded to maximize profits during the last voyage of the season.

Notably, a group of schooners sunk on a pair of reefs in northern Lake Huron offers a dramatic connection between the maritime landscape and the shipwrecks associated with it. Spectacle Reef and nearby Raynold's Reef are a pair of shoals in Lake Huron about 10 miles northeast of Cheboygan. Over the years, scores of vessels have stranded on these shallow water reefs. In 1871, construction began on an

86-foot-tall lighthouse on Spectacle Reef, which was completed in 1874 and still stands today. In September 1869, just prior to construction of the lighthouse, the *Nightingale* (1856-1869) stranded on the reef. Bound from Milwaukee to Oswego with 15,000 bushels of wheat, the schooner *Kate Hayes* (1856-1856) stranded on Spectacle Reef on a clear, calm night in 1856. Nearby are the schooners *Newell Eddy* (1890-1893) and *Augustus Handy* (1855-1861). The 242-foot, three-masted schooner barge *Newell A. Eddy*, built at West Bay City, Mich., in 1890, foundered in a storm with a cargo of grain and all nine hands in 1893. Resting in 160 feet of water, the well-preserved site is a popular dive attraction. In 1855, the *Augustus Handy* was struck by lightning, disabled and sunk.

Smaller schooners, often involved in more local endeavors, are also found in the Thunder Bay area. *Maid of the Mist* (1863-1878; seven-foot depth), for example, was contracted to haul cedar posts from Alpena County to Detroit when it washed ashore in a gale at Huron Beach. Typical of the rough-and-tumble careers of Great Lakes schooners, the 15-year-old vessel was involved in a dozen mishaps before its ultimate demise, and evidence of large-scale repair is preserved in the archaeological record. The 117-foot *William Stevens* (1855-1863; 10-foot depth) and 112-foot *Corsican* (1862-1893; 160-foot depth) are further examples of these smaller-sized schooners, as is the 115-foot *Defiance* (Figure 7, 1848-1854; 185-foot depth), the second-earliest known shipwreck in the area. Remarkably well-preserved with tiller steering and cookstove and galley remnants on deck, *Defiance* is a rare example of an early Great Lakes schooner.

Figure 8. Originally built as a three-masted schooner, the 162-foot *Harvey Bissell* was later retrofitted to a two-masted "schooner barge," a typical conversion for schooners whose owners sought to keep the aging vessels in use. Note the tow line at the bow extending out of the right frame of the photograph. Pictured here with an enormous deck load of lumber, the *Bissell* wreck sits in 15 feet of water just off the Alpena waterfront.

Figures 9 and 10. The wooden steam barge *B.W. Blanchard* operated for 34 years before running aground in Thunder Bay during a blinding snow-storm. With much of the wrecked vessel exposed, it quickly succumbed to winds and waves. Today, its remains lay scattered in shallow water, mixed with the wreckage of other vessels that shared a similar fate.

Larger than canal-size schooners, the 185-foot *American Union* (1862-1894; eight-foot depth) and 150-foot *Portland* (1863-1877; six-foot depth) are both wrecked in shallow water, their deep drafts likely contributing to their demise. Known but yet unidentified remains of another large schooner in shallow water may be the 157-foot *Ishpeming* (1872-1903). In deeper water is the enormous 205-foot *John Shaw* (1885-1895; 118-foot depth), lost off Harrisville in a November snowstorm. Not all wrecking events are dramatic, however. The 162-foot, three-masted schooner *Harvey Bissell* (Figure 8, 1866-1905; 15-foot depth) and canal-sized schooners *Knight Templar* (1965-1903; five-foot depth) and *Light Guard* (1866-1903; six-foot depth), were all abandoned along the inner reaches of Thunder Bay after serving long careers.

Schooners are not the only sailing craft located in the region. The three-masted bark *Ogarita* (1864-1905; 30-foot depth) and brig *Bay City* (1857-1902; 11-foot depth) both wrecked in the sanctuary. *Ogarita* burned and sank when its cargo of 1,200 tons of coal ignited off Thunder Bay Island, while the aging and battered *Bay City* was abandoned along the Alpena waterfront. The two-masted brigantine *John J. Audubon* (1854-1854; 170-foot depth) is located not far from its collision mate, the two-masted schooner *Defiance* mentioned above. Their 1854 collision illustrates the hazards of Great Lakes shipping as it emerged in the mid-19th century. The 1854 shipping season was the most costly to date, with losses totaling 119 lives, 70 ships and $2 million in property. *Defiance* and *John J. Audubon* were among the victims of that dangerous year.

Steamers

Steamers that were purpose-built to carry bulk cargo while simultaneously towing as many as three "consort" barges are well-represented in the sanctuary, particularly on North Point Reef, a geologic feature that extends over one mile from shore and rises to within five feet of the surface. The wooden "steam barge" *Galena* (1857-1872; 16-foot depth) went ashore on North Point carrying 272,000 feet of lumber on Sept. 24, 1872, and quickly broke apart. Much of the machinery, furniture, bedding and crews' possessions were removed from the wreck, and the engine was later salvaged for use in another vessel. Wreckage tentatively identified as the disarticulated pieces of *Galena* lies intermingled with materials from later losses, a common occurrence in the shallow, dynamic waters off North Point Reef.

Photo: Historical Collections of the Great Lakes, Bowling Green State University

Figure 11 (above). The steam barge *Oscar T. Flint* with a schooner barge in tow. Carrying bulk cargo in its own hold, while towing additional barges known as consorts, allowed the steam barge to maximize the amount of cargo conveyed in a single trip. Barges were often aging schooners, as seen here. In 1909, the *Flint* caught fire and sank in 30 feet of water in Thunder Bay.

Photos: NOAA Thunder Bay NMS

Figures 12 and 13 (right top and bottom). Resting in 200 feet of water, the wreck and cargo of the steamer *Florida* is well-preserved. Right: A diver swims between decks, while hovering above are several air-tight barrels still buoyant after 114 years. Above: A view from above into one of the package freighter's cargo holds, with cargo still stacked along the hull.

Similarly, the wooden steam barge *B.W. Blanchard* (Figures 9 and 10), 1870-1904; nine-foot depth) was towing the wooden schooner barges *John T. Johnson* (1873-1904; seven-foot depth) and *John Kilderhouse* when it went aground on North Point during a blinding snowstorm in November 1904. *Blanchard* and *Johnson* were completely wrecked, while *Kilderhouse* was eventually recovered. The vessels carried a combined load of 2,000,000 feet of lumber, most of which was recovered. The suspected *Blanchard* and *Johnson* sites today rest a few hundred feet apart in less than 10 feet of water. Though difficult to identify with precision, the scattered remains of several other vessels are located on North Point Reef as well, including the brig *Empire State* (1862-1877), schooner *E. B. Palmer* (1856-1892) and steamer *Congress* (1861-1868), which saw service during the Civil War in Tidewater, Va. Broken up into several large sections in deeper water off Thunder Bay Island is the steam barge *W. P. Thew* (1884-1909; 70-foot depth), while closer inshore is the steam barge *Oscar T. Flint* (Figure 11, 1889-1909; 30-foot depth), which burned to the waterline and is still filled with its limestone cargo.

With examples spanning over 80 years, bulk and package freighters are also well represented in and around the sanctuary,

including *James Davidson* (1874-1883; 38-foot depth), *Joseph S. Fay* (1871-1905; zero- to 17-foot depth), *D. M. Wilson* (1873-1894; 48-foot depth), *Egyptian* (1873-1897; 230-foot depth), *New Orleans* (1885-1906; 130-foot depth), *W. P. Rend* (1888-1917; 17-foot depth), *Shamrock* (1875-1905; 11-foot depth), *Monohansett* (1872-1907; 18-foot depth), *Florida* (Figures 12 and 13), 1889-1897; 200-foot depth), *Grecian* (1891-1906; 90-foot depth), and *Montana* (Figures 14 and 15), 1872-1914; 60-foot depth). Many of these wrecks are popular dive destinations because of their structural integrity or unique circumstances of loss. *Florida*, for example, collided with the *George W. Roby* off Middle Island and went down with a cargo of 50,000 bushels of wheat, 1,451 barrels and 3,150 sacks of flour, syrup, barrels of whiskey, and a full upper load of package freight, much of which remains on site.

The steel-hulled bulk freight steamer *Grecian*, a Globe Iron Works creation, stranded at De Tour, Mich., then foundered in Thunder Bay while under tow southbound for repairs. Two large steel tanks known as canalons were sunk and fastened to *Grecian's* stern by hardhat divers intending to raise the vessel in 1909. The tanks exploded when filled with air and remain attached to the wreck. *Grecian's* sis-

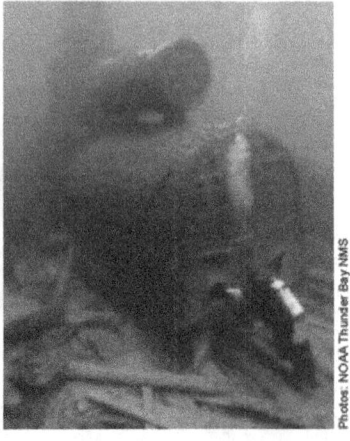

Figures 14 and 15. Launched in 1872, the package freighter *Montana* met her fiery end in Thunder Bay 42 years later — an incredibly long career for a Great Lakes vessel. A typical trip would find the 236-foot *Montana* carrying a diverse cargo of 6,000 barrels of flour, 40 tons of copper, 250,000 shingles, 100 boxes of salmon and some passengers. After 30 years, a changing economy made it important to find new ways to keep the *Montana* profitable. In 1902, the *Montana* began a second career as a "lumber hooker." The cavernous retrofitted vessel now held one million board feet of lumber, enough to stretch for nearly 200 miles if placed end to end.

Figures 16 and 17. The 300-foot-long steamer *Norman* rests in 200 feet of water outside the sanctuary's northern boundary. Listing to port but amazingly intact, the enormous steel wreck contains many artifacts, as well as human remains.

ter ship, the 300-foot-long *Norman* (Figures 16 and 17), 1890-1895; 210-foot depth), is located just 20 miles north, having collided with the Canadian steamer *Jack* in the busy shipping lanes off Presque Isle. Between 1890 and 1920, industrial giants like John D. Rockefeller created steel corporations that required vast Great Lakes fleets to carry iron ore, the main raw material used to make steel. The *Grecian* and *Norman* were part of the fleet serving J. P. Morgan's enormous U.S. Steel Corporation, the nation's first billion-dollar firm.

Perhaps the most tragic accident in Thunder Bay occurred in August 1865, when the passenger freighter *Pewabic* (Figures 18-22), 1863-1865; 160-foot depth) was run into and sunk by its sister vessel *Meteor* with the loss of at least 30 lives. Weather conditions were favorable and the vessels were in sight of one another for several miles before impact. Though injured, *Meteor* was able to continue to Sault Ste. Marie after rescuing many passengers from the water. Built by Peck and Masters of Cleveland, *Pewabic* went down with several

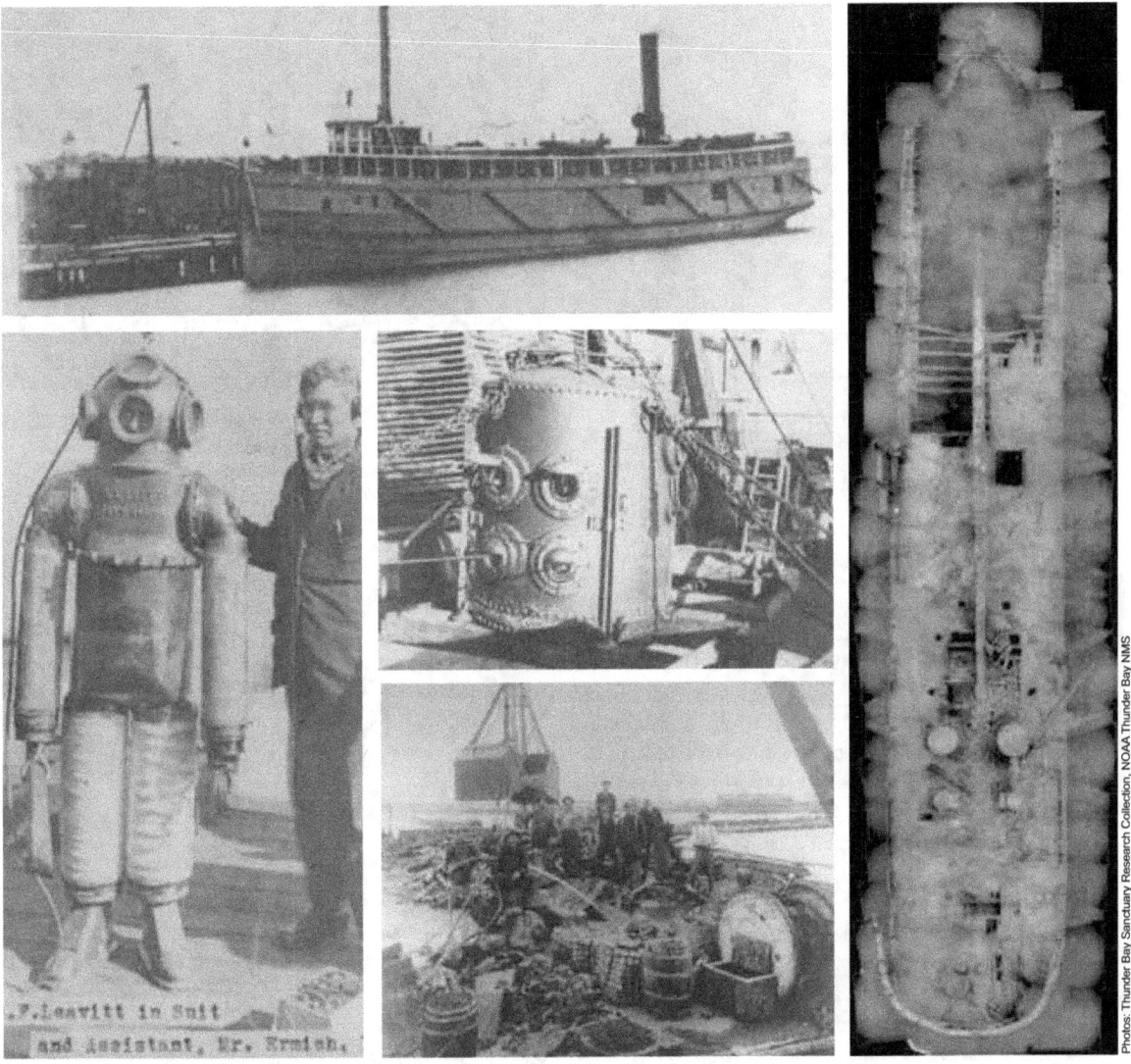

Figures 18-22. The steamer *Pewabic*'s valuable cargo inspired a century of high-risk salvage efforts. Salvors employed divers, dynamite, dredges and even a custom-built diving bell in pursuit of the copper cargo lying 160 feet below the surface. Although these efforts have left an unmistakable, and seemingly negative, imprint at the site, they are actually a part of the shipwreck's history and archaeological record.

hundred tons of valuable copper and iron ore in its hold. Search efforts began immediately, though the wreck was not discovered until June 1897. Much of the cargo was recovered using armored divers, submersible bells with manipulator arms, and bucket cranes, though at great cost; several divers perished on the wreck from drowning or decompression illnesses. At a time when Michigan's Upper Peninsula produced the majority of America's copper, vessels like *Pewabic* were critical to the war effort. The 200-foot steamer raced through

the water at 12 knots, powered by twin engines that turned propellers eight feet in diameter.

Even with more accurate charts and advanced positioning, modern freighters still occasionally sank in Lake Huron during the 20th century. *Isaac M. Scott* (1909-1913; 175-foot depth) was one of eight vessels that sank in Lake Huron during an infamous storm in 1913. The storm took the lives of 194 seamen. The *Scott*, which sank with all hands onboard, lies upside down on the lake bottom like many of its contem-

Figures 23 and 24. Left: The *Monrovia*, pictured here as SS *Commandant Mantelet*, sank during a 1959 collision and became one of the first Great Lakes shipwrecks of the St. Lawrence Seaway era. Linking the Great Lakes to the eastern seaboard via the St. Lawrence River, the final enlargement to the seaway was made in 1959. Over the next 50 years, $350 billion in cargo from more than 50 nations would pass through this engineering marvel. Two other "salties" have wrecked in the Thunder Bay region as well. Right: Today, the wreck of the *Monrovia* sits in 140 feet of water and is a popular dive site.

poraries. *D.R. Hanna* (1906-1919; 130-foot depth), *W.C. Franz* (1901-1934; 230-foot depth), *W. H. Gilbert* (1892-1914; 230-foot depth), *Viator* (1904-1935; 165-foot depth), *Etruria* (1902-1905; 300-foot depth) and *Monrovia* (Figures 23 and 24, 1943-1959; 130-foot depth) all went down resulting from collisions in the busy shipping lanes off Thunder Bay. The German freighter *Nordmeer* (1954-1966; 35-foot depth), Thunder Bay's most recent shipwreck, ran upon a shoal and stuck fast in 1966. The steadfast crew remained onboard for several days hoping to free the freighter, necessitating a daring helicopter rescue by the U.S. Coast Guard amidst a November storm. A local landmark, the vessel's superstructure remained above the waterline for many years until finally succumbing to winter ice and storms and collapsing beneath the surface in 2010. A salvage barge, involved in recovery of scrap steel and machinery from *Nordmeer*, sits on the bottom near the larger wreck.

Perhaps not as romanticized as passenger vessels, paddle wheelers or sailing craft, barges and tugs also played an important role in Great Lakes maritime history. *Lake Michigan Car Ferry Barge No. 1,* built in 1895 by James Davidson to haul 28 rail cars on four tracks across the decks, was converted to a tow barge before sinking with a deck load of lumber and 200 crates of live chickens in November 1918. *Barge No. 83* (1920-1941; 80-foot depth) foundered northeast of Thunder Bay Island with well-drilling machinery and sheet piling. *Haltiner's Barge* (lost 1927; 30-foot depth) sank off North Point with a derrick crane on board, and the *Carbide Barge* (unknown date of loss; 90-foot depth) and *Dump Scow* (unknown date of loss; 130-foot depth) also foundered in heavy seas with unsalvaged deck equipment still in place. Examples of tugs and vernacular craft also exist in and around the sanctuary. The tug *William Maxwell* (1883-1908; 8-foot depth) is visible off Thunder Bay Island in only eight feet of water. Built in Chicago, *Maxwell* was employed by

Figure 25. The tug *W. G. Mason*, built in 1898 and abandoned near Rogers City around 1924. Several smaller, local craft like these are found around Thunder Bay.

the Huron Fish Company to work the waters off Thunder Bay. Today the bilge, deadwood, propeller and shaft of the vessel remain. Off Rogers City are the tugs *W. G. Mason* (Figure 25, 1898-c. 1924; 13-foot depth) and *Duncan City* (1883-c. 1923; 15-foot depth), both excellent snorkel and kayaking sites with consistently clear water.

Maritime Cultural Landscapes

Shipwrecks are not the only submerged cultural resources located in Thunder Bay. Structural features and cultural landscape alterations are also evident on the lake bottom. Cribs, docks, pier footings and pilings are located near the Alpena waterfront, off North Point and around the many islands in the bay. Fishing net stakes, lost navigational aids, refuse and sunken log booms also occur within sanctuary boundaries. Additionally, dozens of vessels were stranded on

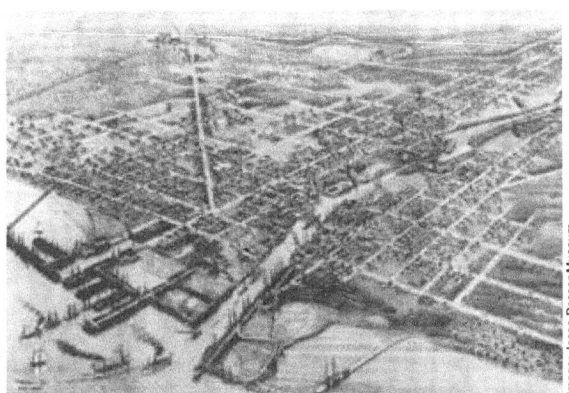

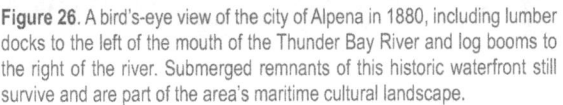

Figure 26. A bird's-eye view of the city of Alpena in 1880, including lumber docks to the left of the mouth of the Thunder Bay River and log booms to the right of the river. Submerged remnants of this historic waterfront still survive and are part of the area's maritime cultural landscape.

various shoals and eventually recovered, leaving behind jettisoned cargo, lost salvage equipment and other artifacts on the lake bottom.

Also significant in number are the shore-side aspects of the region's maritime cultural landscape. As defined by the National Park Service, a cultural landscape is a geographic area including both cultural and natural resources, coastal environments, human communities, and related scenery that is associated with historic events, activities or persons, or exhibits other cultural or aesthetic values (NPS 1997). In addition to the submerged resources described above, maritime cultural landscapes are composed of many shoreline features such as beached shipwrecks, lighthouses, aids to navigation, abandoned docks, working waterfronts and Native American sites (Figures 26 - 28).

Also important are the intangible elements such as spiritual places and legends. A good example is the Native American legend from which Thunder Bay may have derived its name. The story involves We-no-ka, the beautiful daughter of an Ottawa chieftain who favored a Huron brave over would-be Ottawa suitors. While rocking lightly in their canoe one evening, the lovers were beset by a jealous Ottawa brave who fired an arrow at the heart of his rival. We-no-ka heard it first and leapt in front of her lover, only to take the arrow herself and cause the canoe to overturn and drown both of them. The Great Spirit Manitou voiced his displeasure with relentless thunder and lightning, frightening the assassin and sending him to his own death by drowning. From then on, legend has it, no Native American would attempt to cross the Bay of Thunder (Haltiner 2002).

Water

Thunder Bay is located in Lake Huron, which is one of the Great Lakes and part of the world's largest freshwater ecosystem (Franks

Figures 27 and 28. The beached remains of the 215-foot wooden steamer *Joseph S. Fay* (top) and nearby Forty-Mile Point Lighthouse (bottom) are dramatic and closely related aspects of the Thunder Bay area's maritime cultural landscape. Taking on water amidst a violent October storm in 1905, the *Fay*'s captain drove the iron-ore-laden vessel ashore only 200 yards from the lighthouse.

Taylor et al. 2010). Lake Huron is actually four separate but interacting bodies of water: the North Channel, Georgian Bay, Saginaw Bay and Lake Huron proper. The lake is 206 miles in length and a maximum of 183 miles wide (USEPA and Environment Canada 1988). The Lake Huron drainage basin is larger than any other Great Lake's, defined by an expansive watershed that totals 51,700 square miles and an estimated 3,826 miles of shoreline habitat (USEPA and Environment Canada 1988). It is the second-largest of the Great Lakes in area, with approximately 23,000 square miles of surface water, and the third-largest in volume, with 850 cubic miles of water.

The lake is heated significantly in spring, and then heat losses begin to occur over the summer through evaporation (Schertzer 2008). Peak surface temperatures in Thunder Bay are around 72 degrees and generally 68 degrees down to 50 feet. At 80 feet, about nine miles offshore, temperatures range from 40 to 60 degrees, depending on the thermocline, which can vary daily. Below the lowest thermocline, temperatures do not exceed 42 degrees through the year (J. Johnson, MI Dept. of Natural Resources, pers. comm., 2011).

Generally, in December, ice first forms in the bays and other protected areas of Lake Huron. In January, ice forms along the lake perimeter and more exposed shore, and by February, the mid-lake areas typically become frozen (Assel 2003, 2005). Lake Huron's cold, fresh water ensures that Thunder Bay's shipwrecks are among the best-preserved in the world (TBNMS 2009). However, ice and waves are natural processes that can impact exposed or shallow maritime archaeological resources in the sanctuary (see *Pressures* section).

The lake bottom within the sanctuary comprises unique features including several sinkholes in which water composition differs from other areas within the sanctuary. In 2003, water quality studies showed that relative to ambient lake water, water samples that were collected within sinkholes were characterized by slightly higher (4-7.5° C) temperatures, very high levels of chloride and conductivity (10-fold), as well as extremely high concentrations of organic matter, sulfate, and phosphorus. Observations at the submerged sinkholes also demonstrated the occurrence of unique biogeochemical conditions, providing a unique environment for a variety of specialized and uncommon bacteria types (Ruberg et al. 2005).

Habitat

Although some of the habitats have been fragmented and others have been nearly eliminated, in general the Lake Huron watershed basin exhibits a high level of diversity in its natural environments and has retained significant remnants of historic fish and wildlife habitat. This is largely a result of the Lake Huron watershed having a relatively low human population density. The area comprises coastal wetlands (swamps, marshes, bog and fens), islands and rocky shorelines, sand dunes, tributaries, savannahs and prairies. Historically, Lake Huron was connected to stream and inland lake tributaries that provided spawning habitats for many fish species. However, dam and hydroelectric facility construction in the 1800s excluded fish from many of these spawning sites (EPA 2008).

Thunder Bay has a gradually sloping bottom with flats that extend from the nearshore area located off of the Thunder Bay River to the open waters of Lake Huron. Depths range from approximately 25 feet at the eastern boundaries of the nearshore areas to approximately 60 feet at the eastern boundary of Thunder Bay proper (NOAA 1999), although the sanctuary's actual boundaries run further offshore to a maximum depth of 330 feet near the northeast corner, less to the east and southeast. The sanctuary's lake bottom is composed of undifferentiated glacial till (unconsolidated rock materials of all sizes, including clay, silt, sand, gravel and boulders), rocky shoals, limestone walls and various reefs — bedrock exposures that often serve as important spawning habitats. The reef complexes in Thunder Bay are important spawning habi-

[6] For a more general overview see Doermann 2012.

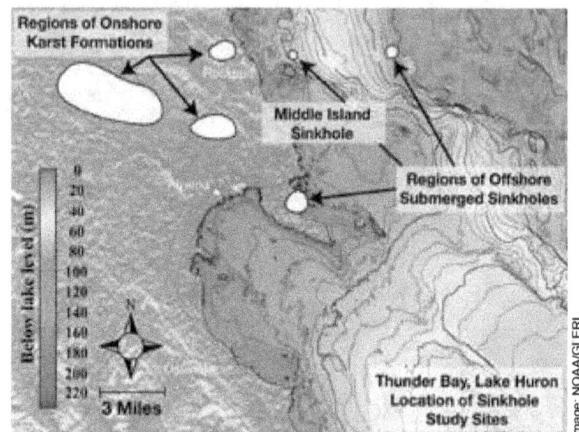

Figure 29. This map shows the locations of offshore karst formations and submerged sinkholes in the Thunder Bay sanctuary.

tats for lake whitefish, walleye and lake trout and are typically heavily colonized by dreissenid mussels (NOAA 1999, EPA 2008, ONMS 2009).

As mentioned above, submerged sinkholes are present in the sanctuary and support a specialized local ecosystem (Figure 29). Thousands of years ago, Lake Huron's limestone bedrock was exposed to extremely low lake levels following the last glacial maximum. Karst sinkholes were created between 10,000 and 8,000 years ago when a chemical reaction between limestone and acidic water dissolved away passages or holes in the rock, leaving behind weakly supported ceilings that could easily collapse or sink. The Lake Huron sinkholes were subsequently covered with water and are currently seeping groundwater to the bottom of the lake, providing a unique habitat for aquatic life. Until recently, it was thought that such unique habitats caused by steep environmental gradients were only found only in oceans. Researchers are now considering the Lake Huron sinkholes to be analogous to marine vent ecosystems — freshwater biogeochemical "hot spots" where nutrients recycle rapidly and where novel organisms and community processes may be observed (Voorhies et al. 2012).[6]

Shipwrecks can also function as marine habitat. Marine studies have shown that although natural reefs tend to have greater overall species richness and abundance, artificial reefs, including shipwrecks, can function as habitat and attract a large diversity and abundance of ecologically and economically valuable species. Furthermore, it has been shown that artificial reefs in coastal habitats can enhance the production of reef-associated species (e.g., macroalgae, invertebrates and fishes) by serving as refuge and foraging grounds (Lindquist et al. 1989, Carr and Hixon 1997). Netting of reefs and observations of fish on shipwrecks by the Michigan Department of Natural Resources show that smallmouth bass and rock bass are the dominant species using both habitat types in warmer, nearshore waters during summer. Walleye use some of the reefs for spawning in spring. Log perch, and especially round gobies, are common prey fishes occupying shallower reefs. The invasive *Hemimysis* has been found to occupy rocky nearshore habitats and perhaps shipwrecks more than other habitat types (MDNR and Central Michigan University, unpublished data). Deeper shipwrecks are less well-studied, but burbot often appear at these sites.

Living Resources

Lake Huron supports a diversity of aquatic plants and organisms, including many rare species, some of which are endemic to the Great Lakes, such as the ebony boghaunter, eastern pond mussel, mudpuppy, eastern fox snake, and piping plover. Recreationally important native fish such as lake trout, lake whitefish, walleye, smallmouth bass, northern pike, and yellow perch are also present. Aquatic animals that may be viewed near shipwrecks include benthic invertebrates such as sponges, hydras, aquatic worms, crayfish, freshwater shrimp, snails, clams, mussels and aquatic insects (Wetzel 1983, Pennak 1989, NOAA 1999).

Aquatic non-indigenous species are also present that can negatively impact ecosystem structure, shipwrecks and other maritime archaeological resources (EPA 2008, ONMS 2009). To date, a comprehensive field study of aquatic plants within the Thunder Bay region has not been completed.

Fish

In general, the fish inhabiting the Thunder Bay region can be characterized as forage and predator species. Important fish stocks in Lake Huron include lake whitefish (*Coregonus clupeaformis*), rainbow smelt (*Osmerus mordax*), bloaters (*Coregonus hoyi*), deepwater sculpin (*Myoxocephalus thompsonii*), slimy sculpin (*Cottus cognatus*), ninespine stickleback (*Pungitius pungitius*), lake herring (*Coregonus artedii*), suckers, and trout-perch (*Percopsis omiscomaycus*) (USFWS 1988, Argyle 1991, NOAA 1999, E. Rutherford, NOAA GLERL and J. Johnson, MI Dept. of Natural Resources, pers. comm., 2012). Most forage species can usually be found inshore near the lake bottom in search of food. Predatory fish species found in Lake Huron include lake trout (*Salvelinus namaycush*), brown trout (*Salmo trutta*), rainbow trout — the anadromous form, known as "steelhead" — (*Oncorhynchus mykiss*), coho salmon (*O. kisutch*), Chinook salmon (*O. tshawytscha*), pink salmon (*O. gorbuscha*), walleye (*Sander vitreus*), yellow perch (*Perca flavescens*) and burbot (*Lota lota*) (USFWS 1988, NOAA 1999 E. Rutherford, NOAA GLERL and J. Johnson, MI Dept. of Natural Resources, pers. comm., 2012). These species can be found in a wide range of depths within inshore and offshore areas of the lake, feeding upon forage fishes. Fish species observed around shipwrecks and other scuba diving sites in the Thunder Bay region include , brown trout, burbot, carp, channel catfish (*Ictalurus punctatus*), northern pike (*Esox lucius*), salmon, smallmouth bass (*Micropterus dolomieu*), steelhead, yellow perch and walleye (War-

A Changing Fish Community

The lake ecosystem has undergone significant changes over the last century, particularly in fish composition, due to changes in the lower food web. Historically, lake trout and burbot were the main fish predators in Lake Huron's deep waters and walleyes were the main nearshore predators. Lake herring, cisco species, sculpins and round whitefish comprised the historic prey fish base. In the 1990s, significant changes to the fish community resulted from overfishing, habitat loss and dam construction. The fish community was also greatly altered by the invasion of various fish species, the most significant of which being rainbow smelt in the 1920s, followed by alewife and the sea lamprey in the 1930s. Sea lamprey predation and overfishing led to the collapse of lake trout in the 1950s in most of Lake Huron. With no predators to control alewife and smelt populations, their numbers rapidly increased. The turnaround came with sea lamprey control in the 1960s, which allowed the survival of stocked Pacific salmon, lake trout and other predators. Restocking has controlled both smelt and alewife populations (EPA 2008). Other recent changes to the food web include the decline in pelagic species such as Chinook salmon, and the restoration of reproductively viable fish species in nearshore areas such as emerald shiner, walleye and yellow perch (Riley et. al., 2008; Fielder et. al., 2007; Johnson 2010). Today, the introduced Pacific salmon have been displaced to a large degree by recovering native predators, walleye and lake trout in particular. The prey base is still composed of a preponderance of nonnative species, led in abundance by rainbow smelt and round gobies (Riley et. al., 2008).

ner and Holecek 1975, NOAA 1999, E. Rutherford, NOAA GLERL and J. Johnson, MI Dept. of Natural Resources, pers. comm., 2012).

Reptiles and Amphibians

Species of reptiles and amphibians recorded for Alpena County that may inhabit the Thunder Bay region include the mudpuppy, Jefferson salamander (*Ambystoma jeffersonianum*), American toad (*Bufo americanus*), wood frog (*Rana sylvatica*), green frog, northern leopard frog (*R.*

pipiens), eastern smooth green snake (*Opheodrys vernalis*), northern water snake (*Nerodia sipedon*), northern brown snake (*Storeria dekayi*), northern ribbon snake (*Thamnophis sauritus*), eastern garter snake (*T. sirtalis*), massasauga rattlesnake (*Sistrurus catenatus*), snapping turtle (*Chelydra serpentina*), and midland painted turtle (*Chrysemys picta marginata*) (Herdendorf et al. 1980, Harding and Holman 1990, NOAA 1999).

Birds

Approximately 160 breeding bird species have been recorded for the Alpena region (Brewer et al. 1991, NOAA 1999, J. Johnson, MI Dept. of Natural Resources, pers. comm., 2012) and include American coot (*Fulica americana*), barn swallow (*Hirundo rustica*), belted kingfisher (*Megaceryle alcyon*), Canada goose (*Branta canadensis*), great blue heron (*Ardea herodias*), green-backed heron (*Butorides virescens*), mallard (*Anas platyrhynchos*), tree swallow (*Tachycineta bicolor*), and wood duck (*Aix sponsa*). The most common colonial nesters on the islands of the bay are ring billed gulls (*Larus delawarensis*), double crested cormorants (*Phalacrocorax auritus*), and herring gulls (*L. smithsonianus*). Winter bird use of Lake Huron is generally low and may include mallard, common goldeneye (*Bucephala clangula*), common merganser (*Mergus merganser*), and red-breasted merganser (*M. serrator*) (USFWS 1988).

Mammals

Mammals that may utilize the coastal wetlands of the Thunder Bay region include eastern cottontail (*Sylvilagus floridanus*), snowshoe hare (*Lepus americanus*), beaver (genus *Castor*), meadow vole (*Microtus pennsylvanicus*), muskrat (*Ondatra zibethicus*), red fox (*Vulpes vulpes*), raccoon (*Procyon lotor*), long-tailed weasel (*Mustela frenata*), mink (*Neovison vison*), river otter (*Lontra canadensis*), and white-tailed deer (*Odocoileus virginianus*) (Herdendorf et al. 1980, NOAA 1999).

Non-indigenous species

As of 2006, at least 200 non-indigenous species have become established in the Great Lakes (Great Lakes Commission 2007). Some of the non-indigenous species in the Thunder Bay region include zebra and quagga mussels (*Dreissena polymorpha* and *D. bugensis*), spiny water flea (*Bythotrephes longimanus*), sea lamprey (*Petromyzon marinus*), round goby (*Neogobius melanostomus*), and white perch (*Morone americana*) (NOAA 1999) and the shrimp-like crustacean known as bloody-red shrimp (*Hemimysis anomala*). Information on the effects of non-indigenous species can be found in later sections of this report (see the *Pressures* section and Question 11).

Pressures on Sanctuary Resources

N atural processes and human activities threaten the long-term sustainability of the Thunder Bay sanctuary's shipwrecks and other maritime archaeological resources. Natural processes such as ice, waves and aquatic invasive species such as zebra and quagga mussels have both known and potential negative impacts on maritime archaeological resources. Human activities have the greatest potential for damaging sanctuary resources. They include anchoring, inadvertent and intentional diving practices that damage resources, and looting. While encouraging increased public access to the unique and irreplaceable shipwrecks of Thunder Bay, the sanctuary strives to balance increased visitation with resource management and preservation. This section describes the nature and extent of the most prominent pressures on Thunder Bay National Marine Sanctuary resources.

Diving and Research

Due to the large number of easily accessible shipwrecks, the area in and around the sanctuary is a popular snorkeling and diving destination. Visiting dive boats and divers have the greatest potential to negatively impact the quality of sanctuary resources. This includes anchor damage to shipwreck sites, leaving temporary mooring lines attached to sites which later become derelict, poor diving practices by divers (e.g., brushing mussels off delicate wood surfaces or handling, moving or inadvertently damaging artifacts), and souvenir hunting and looting (Figures 30 and 31). Substantial damage can occur from anchors, whereby a visiting dive boat "hooks" a shipwreck to both locate the site and secure the boat's anchor.

Due to advances in mixed-gas "technical" and closed-circuit rebreather diving there have been an increased number of divers at deepwater shipwreck sites (130- to 300-foot depths) over the last decade. Generally, shipwrecks at these depths are more intact than shallower sites, due to a less dynamic environment. These sites also possess a greater potential for artifacts to survive, due to the limited — though increasing — number of visitors. Given this, the impacts of looting and anchor damage are relatively greater at these sites. Moreover, new shipwreck discoveries at deeper depths continue to occur. Local shipwreck hunters and divers continue to find remarkably well-preserved shipwrecks at these depths, as does the sanctuary and its partners, who discovered five shipwrecks between 2002 and 2011. Negative impacts from diving at these sites are the same as described above, with potentially greater consequences given that the sites are generally more intact (often with fragile features

Photo: Stan Stock, 2003

Photo: NOAA Thunder Bay NMS, 2011

Figures 30 and 31. Left: The nameboard of the schooner *Kyle Spangler* (1854-1860; 185-foot depth), pictured in 2003, was vivid in its detail. Right: In 2011, the carved relief of the wooden nameboard shows visible signs of wear, as divers have brushed away stubbornly attached quagga mussels to get a photo opportunity.

Figure 34. Moved by divers from their original disposition on the wreck of the steamer *Pewabic*, several artifacts such as copper ingots and ceramic cups and plates have been placed on deck and are more likely to be looted. Although sanctuary regulations and Michigan law prohibit moving artifacts, the practice occurs at many sites where divers want to provide better viewing and photography opportunities. The sanctuary works with the dive community to curb this practice (see *Response* section). Clearly unacceptable is the handling and relocation of human remains, an activity that has been documented at the *Pewabic* site.

Figure 32 and 33. Top: The cabin skylight on the deck of the schooner *Defiance* was in place in 2005. Sometime after the 2005 photo was taken, the fragile skylight was displaced, as indicated in the more recent bottom photo. Whether removed by divers or hooked by a visiting dive boat anchor, the displaced skylight is an indicator of negative human impacts at the site. Note also the diver pushing the tiller, which still moves and articulates the rudder. This type of disturbance is prohibited by state law. Eventually, the 157-year-old tiller will fail, compromising the one-of-a-kind site's substantial recreational, historical and archaeological value. Shipwrecks within the sanctuary are afforded added protection.

Non-indigenous Species

Since the 1800s, human activities have caused the introduction of more than 200 exotic aquatic organisms of all types, including plants, fish, algae and mollusks, in the Great Lakes (Great Lakes Commission 1992, 2007). These species have the potential to cause devastating and often permanent damage to the Great Lakes ecosystem by degrading beaches and swimming areas, changing water quality and clarity, competing with native species for food and habitat, and altering complex food webs that support the aquatic ecosystem (Great Lakes Commission 2007). Of the many invasive species in the Great Lakes, zebra and quagga mussels have had the greatest negative impact on sanctuary resources (Figure 35). Additionally, other invasives that degrade water quality have an indirect effect by potentially limiting physical access to sanctuary resources (e.g., a

preserved) and possess a greater number and variety of artifacts (Figures 32-34).

Archaeological research has the potential to impact sanctuary resources, though to date, documentation conducted by the sanctuary is chiefly non-invasive and carried out "in situ" without moving artifacts or disturbing the site.[7] Occasionally, during the course of an archaeological survey small fasteners are used to attach measuring tapes to sites, but the impact is slight. To date, the sanctuary has not excavated a site or retrieved artifacts, save for a diagnostic cargo sample. In 2005, a small sample of grain cargo was removed from the schooner *Cornelia B. Windiate*, after receiving permission from the Office of the Michigan State Archaeologist. Disturbing, excavating or removing artifacts from a site for research purposes requires a state permit.

Figure 35. Invasive quagga (left) and zebra mussels (right) were introduced into the Great Lakes in the late 1980s.

---

[7] The NOAA Office of National Marine Sanctuaries supports the Annex Rules of the *UNESCO Convention on the Protection of the Underwater Cultural Heritage* (2001). The Annex Rules are a detailed set of guidelines for managing activities directed at underwater cultural heritage based on the International Council on Monuments and Sites Charter on the Protection and Management of Underwater Cultural Heritage (1996). The Annex Rules outline basic principles for the practice of responsible underwater archaeology and provide specific guidance for research, documentation, and artifact curation.

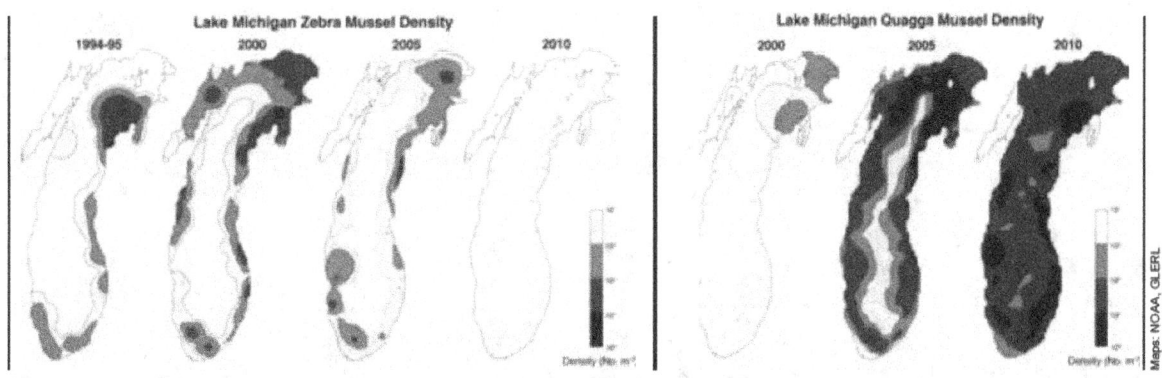

Figure 36. Maps of zebra and quagga mussel distribution over time in Lake Michigan. Note that by 2010, quagga mussels had displaced zebra mussels and are now far more abundant and widespread than zebra mussels ever were. A similar trend is occurring in Lake Huron. Researchers from NOAA's Great Lakes Environmental Lab are studying the trend and in 2012 began an invasive mussel monitoring initiative in Thunder Bay.

beach closure that prevents snorkeling or diving at a near-shore site).

Zebra mussels (*Dreissena polymorpha*) are small, non-indigenous mussels that are native to the Black, Caspian, and Azov seas. However, most likely due to construction of canal systems, they became widespread throughout Europe by the early 19th century. Zebra mussels were first reported in North America in 1988 in the Great Lakes, but likely became established in 1986. The mussels were likely introduced via ballast water of one or more transoceanic ships. Populations first became abundant in Lake St. Clair and western Lake Erie and then spread quickly to all the Great Lakes via intra-basin ballast water exchange and other vectors. Zebra mussels are a very successful invader — they live and feed in many different aquatic habitats, breed prolifically, and have a planktonic larva stage that allows them to drift with currents and spread rapidly. By the early 1990s, zebra mussels became established throughout all five of the Great Lakes (Figure 36), and by the late 1990s were established in the Ohio River Basin and the Mississippi River Basin (Great Lakes Commission 2007, GLERL 2008, MSG 2009a).

Quagga mussels (*Dreissena bugensis*), a close relative of the zebra mussel, are native to the northern portion of the Black Sea. Similar to zebra mussels, their range expanded with the construction of canals throughout Europe. They were first observed in Lake Erie in 1989 and by 2005 had become established throughout the Great Lakes. Like zebra mussels, quagga mussels were most likely introduced into the Great Lakes region from ballast water discharge of transoceanic ships. While zebra mussels are mostly confined to hard objects and substrates, quagga mussels are far more versatile. Unlike zebra mussels, quagga mussels can also live and thrive directly on muddy or sandy bottoms. In addition, quagga mussels can tolerate a wider range of temperatures and water depths than zebra mussels. In particular, they are also highly prolific and capable of spawning in

deeper regions with continuously cold temperatures (MSG 2009b).

Zebra and quagga mussels directly and indirectly affect natural ecosystem functions by altering nutrient cycles and re-engineering physical habitat. Their greatest direct impact is caused by their feeding habits (Vanderploeg et al. 2002, Nalepa et al. 2007, MSG 2009a). They are voracious filter feeders; each mussel is capable of filtering one liter of water per day and removing vast amounts of phytoplankton and suspended particles from the water, thereby depleting the food supply for many native invertebrates found in both the water (zooplankton) and bottom sediments (benthic macroinvertebrates). As a result, these organisms decline in numbers, which in turn has a severe impact on the many fish species that depend on them as a food source. Zebra and quagga mussels attach themselves to any hard surfaces, which includes the shells of native mussels, or unionids. This behavior, called bio-fouling, has greatly reduced populations of native mussels and some other sessile organisms (Gonzalez and Downing 1999, Bially and Macisaac 2000, Nalepa et al. 2007, MSG 2009a). These mussel "reefs" can also dramatically alter water flow regimes by changing the roughness and slope of the benthic habitats.

Zebra and quagga mussels have an affinity for hard surfaces such as boat hulls, engines, docks, buoys, breakwalls, pipelines and submerged archaeological resources (Watzin et al. 2001, MSG 2009a). Therefore, they are a significant nuisance for municipal water treatment plants and power plants. Zebra mussels have the ability to clog water intake valves that are used in pumping stations, electric generating plants, and industrial facilities. Between 1989 and 2004, the cost to control mussels at municipal water plants and power plants in the Great Lakes was about $18 million per year (Connelly et. al., 2007).

The presence of invasive mussels on shipwrecks and other submerged maritime archaeological sites constitutes a significant challenge

Photo: Stan Stock, 2003

Photo: NOAA Thunder Bay NMS, 2008

Figures 37 and 38. Left: Only a few quagga mussels are present in this 2003 image of the anchor stowed on the port rail of the schooner *Kyle Spangler*, resting in 185-feet of water. The variety of wood and iron features, many quite small but still easily made out, are a testament to the preservative qualities of the Great Lakes' cold, fresh water. This high degree of preservation correlates closely to the high archaeological and recreational value of shipwrecks. Right: A 2008 photo shows the same anchor from a similar perspective. Many features are now obscured and have been since 2005. Quagga mussels completely cover the iron shank and flukes, as well as the iron anchor chain. Notably, the two small iron rings, presumably used as part of the apparatus to secure the anchor, are nearly undetectable.

for archaeologists, historians and resource managers, and in many cases reduces a site's archaeological integrity. In terms of detailed archaeological documentation, the baseline has shifted in regards to the quality of data that can be obtained (at least easily) from shipwrecks sites. For example, a timber, feature, or artifact that is encrusted with several inches of mussels will not yield an accurate measurement without removing the covering mussels, an activity that poses its own challenges and is difficult to accomplish over an entire shipwreck site, or even for a representative number of features (Figures 37 and 38).

Research on shipwrecks in Lake Champlain, which has cold, fresh water similar to the Great Lakes, strongly suggests that zebra mussels are accelerating the corrosion of iron fasteners and features of shipwrecks there, probably due to the complex communities of bacteria that accumulate under the thick layers of mussels. Additionally, water quality data definitively document the loss of iron into the water column above the surface of zebra mussel colonies on the wrecks (Watzin et al. 2001). Although the long-term implications of the findings on the structural integrity of shipwrecks is still not clear, it is reasonable to expect that some degree of physical integrity is being lost. Of additional concern is the weight that multiple layers of mussels add to wrecks sites, particularly to pieces of the wreck that may already be loosely attached. Moreover, the total weight of mussels encrusted across an entire shipwreck site can potentially be significant. The weight of mussels has been known to sink submerged buoys, and similar forces are surely at play on shipwreck sites. No-

tably, shipwrecks in depths where limited sunlight and colder water results in less available food were once thought to be beyond the reach of invasive mussels, though since approximately 2003, these sites too have been colonized by quagga mussels.

The public interpretation of shipwreck sites, and perhaps even the public's appreciation for shipwrecks, is also challenged by the presence of thick layers of detail-obscuring mussels. Interestingly, filter feeding mussels have greatly improved water clarity throughout the Great Lakes, presenting a Faustian bargain of sorts. Throughout the Great Lakes, water clarity has increased by 38.5 percent (Higgins and Vander Zander 2010). According to studies by NOAA's Great Lakes Environmental Lab in offshore Lake Michigan, secchi depth[8] was 19.7 feet in 1985-1989, 23 feet in 1995-1998, and 59 feet in 2007-2010. Although quagga mussel numbers are higher in Lake Michigan than Lake Huron, these values give an estimate of the impact mussels can have on water clarity (T. Nalepa, NOAA GLERL, pers. comm., 2012). With quagga mussels now displacing zebra mussels in much of Lake Huron, a similar trend can be expected in and around the sanctuary. Today in Lake Huron, there are seasonal periods where visibility can reach 100 feet, and average visibility in offshore areas is 50 feet or better throughout the year. Prior to invasive mussels in the Lake Huron, visibility rarely exceeded 20 feet and was often less. Consequently, divers, snorkelers, kayakers and tourists on board glass bottom boats now have a far easier time seeing shipwrecks, although the sites are colonized by invasive mussels.

---

[8] Secchi depth measurements are used to determine water transparency and clarity.

Natural Deterioration

Shipwreck sites naturally deteriorate over time, and the speed at which deterioration occurs is determined by environmental conditions. The presence of salt versus fresh water, certain marine organisms, warm versus cold water, bottom sediment type, water depth, the potential for ice formation, and other local geographical and environmental factors all contribute to the natural deterioration of shipwrecks. As mentioned previously, the cold, freshwater environment of Lake Huron helps preserve sanctuary shipwrecks by inhibiting marine organisms harmful to shipwrecks and slowing corrosion that occurs in marine environments. However, ice movement, currents, shifting sediments, storms and normal wave action are all environmental factors that can be detrimental to shipwrecks, particularly those in shallow depths (Figures 39 – 42).

Generally, as depth increases, so too does the structural integrity of shipwrecks in and around Thunder Bay due to the less dynamic environment at depth (Figure 43). However, other factors such as the circumstances of a vessel's sinking can offset the potential for increased structural integrity at increasing depths. For example, a vessel that burned to the waterline or collided with another vessel before sinking may have reduced structural integrity once it comes to rest on the bottom, thereby setting the stage for an accelerated pace of

natural deterioration. Conversely, a vessel that founders and comes to rest on the bottom intact will generally survive much better in deep water than shallow water. Constituent components such as hull, deck and cabin construction materials (wood versus steel or iron) also play a role in how natural degradation plays out at a shipwreck site.

Individual artifacts may survive well in both shallow and deep-water environments. At shallower sites with loose sediment, smaller artifacts may be dispersed, thus losing their archaeological context; however, they can also become physically protected by being buried in the lake bottom. Buried artifacts can also benefit from a low-oxygen environment, which slows deterioration. Shallow sites located on cobble or hard bottom understandably have a lesser chance of being preserved in sediment, though here too some artifacts will survive. At deeper depths, artifacts typically have a higher likelihood of surviving in their original positions, offering a clearer context. It is not uncommon for an entire complement of deck hardware (windlass, pumps, winches, etc.) to remain fixed in their original positions, or for personal effects and smaller artifacts to remain in localized areas such as a deck cabin. Here too, fresh water helps preserve artifacts, even those not buried in protective sediments. Paper, leather, bone and other organic artifacts can survive remarkably well in fresh water. Glass, ceramic, wooden

Figures 39 and 40. The shipwreck *Nordmeer* (1954-1966; 35-foot depth) rests on Thunder Bay Island Shoal, where ice and waves have battered the steel vessel for 44 years. The image at left was taken just after the vessel ran aground. By 2010, only a small portion of the vessel remained above the surface (right), but this too finally succumbed to natural processes, leaving the entire wreck today collapsed below the water's surface.

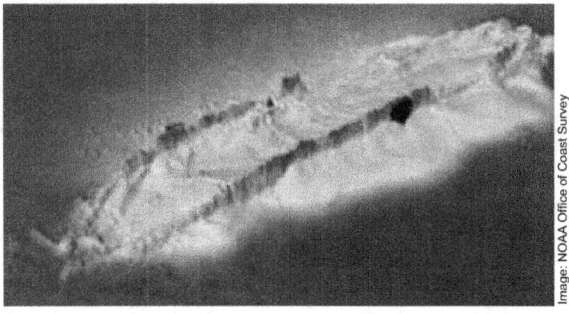

Figures 41 and 42. The 287-foot-long steamer *W.P. Rend* (1888-1917; 17-foot depth), above left, ended its long career in the shallow water of Thunder Bay's inner reaches. The multibeam sonar image above right reveals the effects of natural degradation on this shallow water shipwreck site.

Image: NOAA Thunder Bay NMS/Robert McGreevy

Photo: NOAA Thunder Bay NMS

Figure 43. A perspective view of the wooden schooner *Kyle Spangler*, resting in 185 feet of water. Largely intact, except for collision damage at the bow, the site represents the high degree of preservation of many shipwrecks in this depth range. In 2008, sanctuary archaeologists worked with the wreck's founder, Michigan diver Stan Stock, to document the site.

Figure 44. In this 2009 image, commercial fishing gear can be seen snarled around the frames of the steamer *O. E. Parks*. A decline in commercial gillnetting and greater awareness as to the locations of sanctuary shipwrecks has led to a decrease in new gear being snagged on sanctuary resources.

and metal artifacts are often found in excellent states of preservation. Many of these types of materials occur in and around the sanctuary.

There are potential links between climate change in the Great Lakes and the deterioration of shipwrecks, but research has not been done on the topic, and questions remain. For example, should climate change result in significantly decreased ice coverage on the Great Lakes, this would enhance evaporation and lead to a water level decline. As water levels drop, shallow water shipwrecks may become more exposed to air, waves and ice, thus accelerating natural decomposition. Nearshore shipwrecks in sandy lakebed environments may suffer increased deterioration as increasingly mobile sediment (due to a more dynamic environment created by lower water levels) variously exposes and buries sites. Moreover, the sudden occurrence of a shallow-water shipwreck exposed by shifting sediment makes for an exciting discovery, but one that is also potentially very accessible, and can lead to both intentional and unintentional human impacts. The effects of climate change on a delicately balanced and already stressed ecosystem could also have negative impacts by reducing water quality and, consequently, public accessibility to sanctuary resources.

Fishing and Boating

The groups using the Lake Huron fisheries are state licensed commercial fishers, recreational anglers, and Native American commercial fishers. Great Lakes commercial fishing has declined significantly since the 1940s, when commercial fish stocks collapsed. In 1930, close to 7,000 people were employed in the commercial fishing industry, but by 1975, a little over 1,100 people were employed. Since 2001, only two state-licensed and two to four tribally licensed commercial fishing operations have been operating out of Alpena County.

Gillnets are no longer permitted for commercial fishing in central and southern Lake Huron, including within the sanctuary boundaries; trapnets are the only gear used. Today, the Thunder Bay region of Lake Huron is considered one of the most lucrative whitefish fishing grounds in the Great Lakes, and whitefish is the principal commercially harvested species within the Thunder Bay region (NOAA 1999). In 2000, about 60% of all lake whitefish came from Lake Huron (Kinnunen 2003). This decrease in commercial fishing has led to less impact from fishing gear at shipwreck sites.

In contrast, the popularity of recreational fishing has increased over the last century, particularly since the late 1960s, when salmon was introduced in the Great Lakes (NOAA 1999). In 1975, approximately 2.8 million recreational anglers were active on the Great Lakes (U.S. Comptroller General 1977). In 2006, 1.4 million persons age 16 years and older participated in recreational fishing in the U.S. waters of the Great Lakes, taking 13.3 million trips during 18 million days on the water and spending $1.5 billion on equipment and trip-related items (USFWS and U.S. Dept. of Commerce Census Bureau 2007). Recreational fishing primarily targets lake trout, brown trout, steelhead, walleye and salmon. Popular fishing techniques include the use of planer boards and downriggers to take fishing line to specified depths. With the downturn in Chinook salmon numbers after 2004, there has been a 73% reduction in recreational fishing pressure in the Main Basin of Lake Huron. Walleyes are now the leading target for recreational fishing in Thunder Bay (Johnson and Gonder, in press).

Commercial and recreational fishing and boating are potential stressors to sanctuary maritime archaeological resources, with the biggest threat being damage resulting from deploying, dragging and recovering anchors and nets (Figure 44). Although impacts from fishing lures from trolling is possible (e.g., drifting and anchored fishing boats can become snagged in wrecks sites and potentially damage a fragile site), the potential impact is slight. Derelict lines and lures pose a potential hazard to scuba divers. Although gillnet remnants are known to exist at a couple shipwreck sites in the sanctuary, the future threat is not great given the limited number of commercial fishers in the area and the prohibition of gillnets in U.S. waters of Lake Huron south of Hammond Bay. In addition, the remaining Native American and commercial fishermen avoid known wreck sites, as they are hazards to fishing gear.

Pressures on Water Quality

The following outlines pressures on water quality that can impact submerged archaeological resources in the sanctuary, chiefly by reducing public accessibly.

Nonpoint Sources of Pollution

Unlike point source pollution[9], nonpoint source pollution comes from many diffuse sources. Nonpoint source water pollution is usually due to rainfall moving over and through the ground and carrying various chemicals. As the runoff moves, it picks up and carries away pollutants, finally depositing them into surface and subsurface (groundwater) waters. Pollutants and contaminants include excess fertilizers, herbicides and insecticides from agricultural lands and residential areas; oil, grease and toxic chemicals from urban runoff and energy production; sediment from improperly managed construction sites and dredging operations; bacteria and nutrients from birds and other wildlife; pet wastes; and faulty septic systems. Eutrophication (an outcome of excess nutrients in the water, such as fertilizers) of nearshore waters has been an ongoing, documented problem in some nearshore waters of Lake Huron. The process of eutrophication has the potential to shift primary productivity from the slower-growing flora (e.g., grasses) to faster-growing species (e.g., algae) (Fourqurean et al. 2003, Wagner et al. 2008). While the eutrophication rate from the watershed is apparently very low, dreissenid mussels have concentrated the lake's nutrients in the nearshore zone and on the lake bottom (Hecke et al). This has favored colonial, benthic algae such as *Cladophora*, which can tap into these benthic resources and are not eaten by dreissenids. Blue-green algae (cyanobacteria) are another beneficiary of this nearshore shunt of nutrients. Most blue-green algae are also not edible by dreissenids. These changes have actually increased water clarity during most months, except when blue-green blooms occur.

Harmful Algal Blooms

A harmful algal bloom (HAB) can occur when certain types of microscopic algae grow quickly in water, forming visible patches that may harm the health of the environment, plants, or animals. HABs are attributed to two primary factors: natural processes such as warm water and poor water circulation and flow, and anthropogenic causes such as nutrient loading leading to eutrophication. These processes can result in large amounts of certain types of phytoplankton (e.g., blue-green algae) accumulating in the water. Aggregations of these organisms can discolor the water, thus making shipwrecks less visible. In addition, some HAB-causing algae can release toxins into the water that adversely impact aquatic organisms and humans. Impacts include fish kills and skin and respiratory problems in humans. HABs have occurred in the waters of almost every U.S. coastal state. Over the last several decades, HABs have caused more than $1 billion in economic losses in the U.S. due to closures of shellfish beds and coastal fisheries, detrimental impacts on tourism and service industry revenues, and public illnesses (Abbott et al. 2009). Data suggests that HABs are increasing in frequency within the last couple of decades (Harvell et al. 1999). Beach closures due to HABs can impact the public's access to sanctuary resources.

Beach Closures

Runoff and spills have periodically resulted in high levels of *Escherichia coli* (*E. coli*) bacteria in the sanctuary, resulting in beach closures. *E. coli* is often used as an indicator organism in nearshore water quality monitoring, and while it may not always cause diseases in humans, its presence can indicate that water may be contaminated with organisms that cause human health impacts such as fever,

While the Lake Huron watershed is home to about 2.5 million people, both sides of Lake Huron have relatively low human population densities. The Lake Huron basin contains no major metropolitan areas. The largest urban centers in the basin are Sudbury and Sault Ste. Marie on the Ontario side and Flint, Saginaw and Bay City on the Michigan side. With populations under 120,000, these urban areas are relatively small compared to urban areas in the more populous Great Lake basins (EPA 2008).

---

[9] Point source pollution results when a pollutant is discharged direcly into surface waters from a definite locaion, such as the pipes of industrial waste facilities or domesic sewage treatment plants.

flu-like symptoms, ear infection, respiratory illness, rashes, gastroenteritis, cryptosporidiosis, and hepatitis. Sources of polluted and contaminated water include runoff from urban, suburban and rural areas, aging sewer infrastructure systems pressed to meet increasing demands, and contaminated flows from other upland sources.

Contributing factors that generate these sources include illicit storm drain connections, improper disposal of materials or maintenance that clog pipes and cause overflows, cracked or damaged pipes, overflow of sewer systems during storm events, septic system leaching, and various domestic and wildlife sources.

State of Sanctuary Resources

This section provides summaries of the condition and trends within four resource areas: water, habitat, living resources and maritime archaeological resources. For each, sanctuary staff and selected outside experts considered a series of questions about each resource area. The set of questions derive from the National Marine Sanctuary System's mission, and a system-wide monitoring framework (NMSP 2004) developed to ensure the timely flow of data and information to those responsible for managing and protecting resources in the ocean and coastal zone, and to those that use, depend on, and study the ecosystems encompassed by the sanctuaries. The questions are meant to set the limits of judgments so that responses can be confined to certain reporting categories that will later be compared among all sanctuary sites and combined. The Appendix (Rating Scheme for System-Wide Monitoring Questions) clarifies the set of questions and presents statements that were used to judge the status and assign a corresponding color code on a scale from "good" to "poor." These statements are customized for each question. In addition, the following options are available for all questions: "N/A" – the question does not apply; and "undetermined" – resource status is undetermined. In addition, symbols are used to indicate trends: "▲ " – conditions appear to be improving; "▬" – conditions do not appear to be changing; "▼ " – conditions appear to be declining; and "?" – the trend is undetermined.

This section of the report provides answers to the set of questions. Answers are supported by specific examples of data, investigations, monitoring and observations, and the basis for judgment is provided in the text and summarized in the table for each resource area. Where published or additional information exists, the reader is provided with appropriate references and Web links.

Judging an ecosystem as having "integrity" implies the relative wholeness of ecosystem structure and function, along with the spatial and temporal variability inherent in these characteristics, as determined by the ecosystem's natural evolutionary history. Ecosystem integrity is reflected in the system's ability to produce and maintain adaptive biotic elements. Fluctuations of a system's natural characteristics, including abiotic drivers, biotic composition, complex relationships, and functional processes and redundancies are unaltered and are either likely to persist or be regained following natural disturbance.

Not all questions, however, use ecosystem integrity as a basis for judgment. One focuses on the impacts of water quality factors on human health. Another rates the status of key species compared with that expected in an unaltered ecosystem. One rates maritime archaeological resources based on their historical, archaeological, scientific and educational value. Another considers the level and persistence of localized threats posed by degrading archaeological resources. Finally, four ask specifically about the levels of ongoing human activity that could affect resource condition.

Thunder Bay National Marine Sanctuary regulations specify the management of cultural resources. Therefore, the sanctuary manages shipwrecks and related maritime archaeological resources, and not ecological resources. Consequently, this condition report does not directly address other aspects of the ecosystem. Specifically, Questions 5, 6, 7 and 8 relating to Habitat and Questions 9, 10, 12 and 13 relating to Living Resources were deemed not applicable due to the scope of sanctuary management regulations and therefore, responses to these questions have not been provided. Exceptions, however, occur when the natural resource-based questions can be addressed in the context of how that ecosystem element impacts maritime archaeological resources and the public's access to these resources. For this reason, Questions 1, 2, 3 and 4 relating to Water Quality are answered, as are Questions 11 and 14 relating to non-indigenous species. A text box provides a general overview of the condition and trends of ecological resources in the sanctuary, as determined by agencies other than the sanctuary.

Although its regulations specify the management of cultural resources, the Thunder Bay sanctuary promotes and facilitates a broad spectrum of natural resource research (see *Response to Pressures* section). From real-time weather observation and instrumentation to artificial reefs to the chemistry and microbiology of submerged sinkholes, the sanctuary's research efforts seek to better understand the natural aspects of northern Lake Huron. The sanctuary's role in this natural resource research is evolving and expanding. Consequently, future condition reports may seek to address natural resources as stand-alone questions.

The Sweetwater Sea: Strategies for Conserving Lake Huron Biodiversity

In 2010, the Nature Conservancy (TNC) in Michigan released a report titled, "The Sweetwater Sea: Strategies for Conserving Lake Huron Biodiversity" (Franks Taylor et al. 2010). This report, developed through a two-year planning process involving more than 400 individuals from more than 100 agencies and organizations from around the Lake Huron basin, summarizes the condition and long-term outlook of Lake Huron. The report describes Lake Huron as an ecologically rich and globally significant ecosystem; however, its biodiversity is at risk. The most critical threats to Lake Huron's biodiversity were identified as non-native invasive aquatic and terrestrial species, climate change, rapid and poorly planned residential and industrial growth, altered shorelines and hydrology (e.g., dams and barriers), and agricultural, forestry and urban non-point source pollution.

Status ratings were assigned to seven key biodiversity features:

- *Open water benthic and pelagic ecosystem (open water ecosystem beyond the 30-meter bathymetric contour from the mainland or islands, including reefs and shoals): FAIR*

- *Nearshore zone (submerged lands and water column of Lake Huron starting at zero meters in depth and extending to 30 meters in depth, not including areas upstream from river mouths and riverine coastal wetlands): FAIR*

- *Islands (land masses within Lake Huron that are surrounded by water, including artificial islands that are 'naturalized' or support nested targets. Nested feature examples: colonial nesting waterbirds, globally rare species, migratory bird stopover sites): GOOD*

- *Native migratory fish (native fish that migrate to and depend on tributaries, nearshore areas, or wetlands as part of their natural life cycles): FAIR*

- *Coastal wetlands (all types of wetlands with historic or current hydrologic connectivity to, and directly influenced by Lake Huron: FAIR*

- *Coastal Terrestrial System (natural communities from the line of wave action to two kilometers inland): FAIR*

- *Aerial Migrants (migrating species with high fidelity to Lake Huron, and for which migratory corridors and stopover habitat associated with the lake are crucial to their survival): FAIR*

The ratings used by TNC were as follows:

- *Very Good – the indicator is functioning at an ecologically desirable status and requires little human intervention.*

- *Good – the indicator is functioning within its acceptable range of variation; it may require some human intervention.*

- *Fair – the indicator lies outside its acceptable range of variation and requires human intervention. If unchecked, the target will be vulnerable to serious degradation.*

- *Poor – allowing the indicator to remain in this condition for an extended period will make restoration or preventing extirpation practically impossible.*

A copy of the full report may be downloaded from http://conserveonline.org/workspaces/lakehuron.bcs/documents.

Water

1. Are specific or multiple stressors, including changing oceanographic and atmospheric conditions, affecting water quality and how are they changing?

This question is rated "good/fair" because selected conditions may degrade maritime archaeological resources and reduce the public's access to these resources, but are not likely to cause substantial or persistent declines. The trend is "undetermined."

Water quality in Lake Huron has been strongly influenced by invasive zebra and quagga mussels. These mussels occur at high densities, filter large water volumes while feeding on suspended materials, and deposit particulate waste on the lake bottom. Because phosphorus is associated with suspended particulate matter, mussels located in shallow, nearshore areas are believed to sequester phosphorus from tributaries before it can be transported offshore. Phosphorus is the limiting nutrient for primary production; therefore, nearshore areas are experiencing enhanced eutrophication and its effects, including deposits of filamentous benthic algae on beaches and algal blooms, which in turn can limit public access to sanctuary resources. In contrast, however, offshore areas are experiencing starvation symptoms such as pronounced declines of zooplankton and benthic invertebrate communities and a collapse of the demersal fish community. This assessment applies generally to Lake Huron, but is applicable to Thunder Bay. Although eutrophication does not directly impact shipwrecks, the presence of invasive mussels does (see Question 11 for additional explanation regarding the impact of invasive mussels on sanctuary resources).

Changing atmospheric conditions can potentially impact sanctuary resources, though the range and significance of these changes has not been well studied. Several potential direct connections likely exist. For example, in Lake Huron there has been an average yearly decline in ice cover of 1.64%, resulting in a 62% total ice loss over the last 38 years (Wang et al. 2011). Researchers have noted that decreased ice coverage enhanced evaporation and led to a significant water level decline of as much as three to four feet (varies by lake) from the early 1990s to the early 2000s (Sellinger et al. 2008). Decreasing water levels present a range of potential negative impacts to sanctuary resources, including exposing sites that were previously submerged.

Research is needed to better understand the extent to which changing atmospheric conditions, including climate change, could impact sanctuary resources. Similarly, atmospheric conditions that trigger changes in Lake Huron's water quality may indirectly affect sanctuary resources by impacting public visitation and archaeological research at shipwreck sites.

2. What is the eutrophic condition of sanctuary waters and how is it changing?

This question is rated "fair" because selected conditions may cause measurable but not severe declines in maritime archaeological resources and possibly the public's access to these resources, as well. However, eutrophication from the Thunder Bay watershed is currently low and not growing appreciably because human population growth in the area is near zero and there are recent changes in laws governing land application of phosphorus. Additionally, reservoirs trap nutrients coming down the Thunder Bay River and the watershed still is largely forested or in pasture, and dreissenid effects appear to be declining. Therefore the trend is "not changing." However, given the poor eutrophic conditions in other areas of the Great Lakes and the dynamic nature of Thunder Bay, the potential effects of change in condition are summarized briefly below.

Eutrophication resulting from excessive nutrient loads generally promotes excessive algae growth (harmful algal blooms) and decay, thus causing a disruption in the normal function of the ecosystem. Water quality can be severely reduced and will usually become cloudy and discolored, thus potentially impacting sanctuary resources and the public's access to them (e.g., reduced visibility; algal blooms can result in beach closures). In the Great Lakes, eutrophication is often associated with green algae (*Cladophora*) and blue-green algae (cyanobacteria) blooms that are capable of drastically altering benthic conditions. These algal blooms are likely due to multiple factors, including inadequate municipal wastewater and residential septic systems; runoff from increased impervious surface areas and agricultural row-crop areas; discharges from tile drainage, which result in more dissolved reactive phosphorus loading; industrial livestock operations; ecosystem changes from invasive mussel species; and impacts from climate change, which include warmer water and more frequent and intense precipitation and stormwater events (International Joint Commission 2011).

In the past 5 to 10 years, excessive *Cladophora* growth in parts of the Great Lakes has re-emerged as a management problem. A 2004 workshop held at the Great Lakes WATER Institute at the University of Wisconsin-Milwaukee noted that "[*Cladophora*] has resulted in public complaint, generally related to the decline in aesthetic conditions near the lakeshore. Other negative impacts include human health hazards (e.g., *Cladophora* mats may promote the growth or retention of pathogens), the clogging of water intakes (including those of power plants), the loss of recreation opportunities, and declining lakefront property values. In addition to direct impacts on humans, excessive *Cladophora* growth may have significant impacts on ecosystem functions and properties such as nutrient cycling, energy flow and food web structure" (Bootsma et al. 2004). Although algal blooms do not directly impact sanctuary resources, algal blooms that lead to beach closures and reduced water clarity could negatively impact the public's access to shipwrecks. Although eutrophication from the watershed appears to be less in the Thunder Bay area than at many other locations in the Great Lakes, *Cladophora* is indeed a problem, and nearshore shunt of nutrients is thought to be the leading cause (Hecky et. al. 2004).

3. Do sanctuary waters pose risks to human health and how are they changing?

This question is rated as "good/fair" because selected conditions that have the potential to affect human health, and thereby impact the public's access to sanctuary resources, may exist, but human impacts have not been reported. The trend is "not changing."

Escherichia coli (*E. coli*) is often used as an indicator organism in nearshore water quality monitoring, and its presence can indicate that the water may be contaminated and health impacts such as fever, flu-like symptoms, ear infection, respiratory illness, rashes, gastroenteritis, cryptosporidiosis and hepatitis can occur. As such, county health departments in Michigan regularly monitor levels of *E. coli* in waters adjacent to public beaches and compare levels against state water quality standards. When *E. coli* levels exceed guidelines set by the state, swimming advisories are issued and beaches are closed for swimming. Beaches are only reopened when *E. coli* levels fall within acceptable levels again.

The Michigan Department of Natural Resources and Environment's "BeachGuard" database includes 14 beaches in Alpena County. Two of the Lake Huron beaches in the city of Alpena had closures in 2009 and 2010, and one had a closure in 2011 (http://www.deq.state.mi.us/beach/BeachDetail.aspx?BeachID=285):

Blair Street

- 2009: One day of closure (8/18-19, 2009) for high bacteria levels due to stormwater runoff.

- 2010: Three days of closure (8/18-19, 2010) for high bacteria levels due to stormwater runoff and 8/10-12/10 for rainfall due to stormwater runoff.

Starlite Beach

- 2010: Two days of closure (8/10-12, 2010) for high bacteria levels due to stormwater runoff

Michekewis Beach

- 2011: One day of closure (6/23-24, 2011) for high bacteria levels due to stormwater runoff

Harmful algal blooms (HABs) are becoming an increasing problem in the Great Lakes. While HABs are more prevalent in Lake Michigan and Lake Erie, there are incidents of HABs on the Thunder Bay shoreline. HABs can cause fishkills that can wash up on shore and produce harmful conditions to marine life as well as humans. In addition, blue-green algae (cyanobacteria)

can produce skin irritants under certain conditions, and some can produce multiple types of harmful toxins. These issues could potentially limit recreational access to sanctuary resources.

4. What are the levels of human activities that may influence water quality and how are they changing?

This question is rated as "good/fair" because some potentially harmful activities exist, but they do not appear to have had a negative effect on water quality, thus there is minimal impact to public access of sanctuary maritime archaeological resources. The trend is "improving."

Human activities that may influence water quality include both point and nonpoint source pollution. The Thunder Bay River watershed has relatively few point source pollutant sources. Few factories and wastewater treatment plants are in the watershed, with only six permitted discharges in the basin. Recent surveys by the Michigan Department of Environmental Quality (MDEQ) indicate that most of the Thunder Bay watershed is meeting state water quality standards.

As mentioned previously, poor water quality has the potential to limit recreational use of sanctuary resources. At this time, however, the human activities that influence water quality do not appear to have had a negative effect on water quality.

Water Quality Status & Trends

#	Issue	Rating	Basis for Judgment	Description of Findings
1	Stressors	?	Invasive zebra and quagga mussels have altered water quality; ice coverage has declined and water levels have fluctuated. Changes in water quality could negatively impact public access to sanctuary resources.	Selected conditions may degrade maritime archaeological resources, but are not likely to cause substantial or persistent declines.
2	Eutrophic Condition	—	Algal blooms that lead to beach closures and reduced water quality could negatively impact the public's access to sanctuary resources.	Selected conditions may cause measurable but not severe declines in maritime archaeological resources.
3	Human Health	?	Documented swimming advisories and beach closures may limit the public's access to sanctuary resources.	Selected conditions that have the potential to affect human health may exist but human impacts have not been reported.
4	Human Activities	▲	Few point sources, however, nonpoint source pollution can occur after heavy rain. Poor water quality could limit the public's access to sanctuary resources.	Some potentially harmful activities exist, but they do not appear to have had a negative effect on water quality.

Status: Good Good/Fair Fair Fair/Poor Poor Undet.

Trends: Improving (▲), Not Changing (—), Declining (▼), Undetermined Trend (?), Question not applicable (**N/A**)

Habitat

5. *What is the abundance and distribution of major habitat types and how is it changing?*

Thunder Bay National Marine Sanctuary regulations specify the management of only maritime archaeological resources. For this reason, this question was deemed "not applicable."

6. *What is the condition of biologically structured habitats and how is it changing?*

Thunder Bay National Marine Sanctuary regulations specify the management of only maritime archaeological resources. For this reason, this question was deemed "not applicable."

7. *What are the contaminant concentrations in sanctuary habitats and how are they changing?*

Thunder Bay National Marine Sanctuary regulations specify the management of only maritime archaeological resources. For this reason, this question was deemed "not applicable."

8. *What are the levels of human activities that may influence habitat quality and how are they changing?*

Thunder Bay National Marine Sanctuary regulations specify the management of only maritime archaeological resources. For this reason, this question was deemed "not applicable."

Habitat Status & Trends

#	Issue	Rating	Basis for Judgment	Description of Findings
5	Abundance/Distribution	N/A		N/A
6	Structure	N/A	Thunder Bay National Marine Sanctuary regulations specify the management of only maritime archaeological resources. For this reason, Questions 5 - 8 were deemed "not applicable."	N/A
7	Contaminants	N/A		N/A
8	Human Activities	N/A		N/A

Status: Good Good/Fair Fair Fair/Poor Poor Undet.

Trends: Improving (▲), Not Changing (—), Declining (▼), Undetermined Trend (?), Question not applicable (**N/A**)

Living Resources

9. *What is the status of biodiversity and how is it changing?*

Thunder Bay National Marine Sanctuary regulations specify the management of only maritime archaeological resources. For this reason, this question was deemed "not applicable."

10. *What is the status of environmentally sustainable fishing and how is it changing?*

Thunder Bay National Marine Sanctuary regulations specify the management of only maritime archaeological resources. For this reason, this question was deemed "not applicable."

11. *What is the status of non-indigenous species and how is it changing?*

Non-indigenous species in the sanctuary, particularly zebra and quagga mussels, have caused or are likely to cause declines in the integrity of maritime archaeological resources. For this reason, the response to this question is rated "poor." The rate that mussels may be impacting resources is very slow and not comprehensively documented in the sanctuary, but the impact is negative and irreversible. Due to uncertainty regarding future changes in non-indigenous species dynamics and their impacts on sanctuary resources, the trend is "undetermined."

Zebra and quagga mussels (dreissenids) are highly concentrated near the mouth of the Thunder Bay River, which enters Thunder Bay at the city of Alpena (Black et al. 2000). Because zebra and quagga mussels have an affinity for hard substrates, they are commonly found attached to submerged maritime archaeological resources. When first introduced into the Great Lakes in the 1980s, zebra and quagga mussels first colonized shallow, well-lit shipwreck sites. Today, however, sanctuary archaeologists have observed significant quagga mussel infestation on shipwrecks sites as deep as 300 feet (R. Green, TBNMS, pers. obs.). Although dreissenids settle on all hard substrates, it has been documented that they appear to prefer wrought iron and steel surfaces (Watzin et al. 2001). As a result, there is concern over the effects of the spread of dreissenid colonization on shipwrecks. The latest lake-wide survey of quagga mussels, which included sites within the sanctuary, showed that mussel abundances increased two-fold between 2003 and 2007 at depths greater than 50 meters, and about four-fold at depths between 51 and 90 meters (T. Nalepa, NOAA GLERL, unpub. data).

The initial impact of dreissenid attachment is the loss of "archaeological visibility" — the surfaces of a historic shipwreck can literally disappear under layers of mussels (Kraft 1996, Watzin et al. 2001). While the shape of the shipwreck is still recognizable, the details of its surface and construction are obscured,

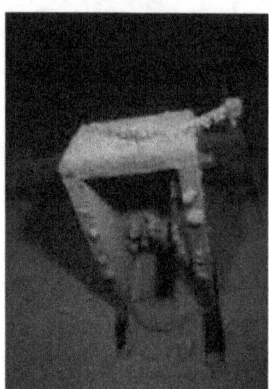
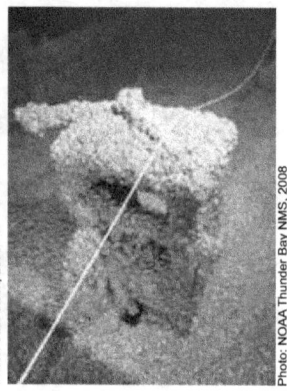

Photo: Stan Stock, 2003

Photo: NOAA Thunder Bay NMS, 2008

Figures 45 and 46. Left: A 2003 photo of the centerboard winch on board the schooner *Kyle Spangler*. Sunk in 1860, the wooden ship lies in 180 feet of water in northern Lake Huron. Some mussels are present, but all of the winch's details are still visible. Right: A 2008 photo of the same winch (though opposite side), covered with a thick layer of quagga mussels. The difficulty of archaeologically documenting the winch is dramatically apparent, as is the potential for decreased recreational value.

thus severely impacting the potential for detailed study of these resources (Figures 45 and 46). Infestation of dreissenids could also diminish the interest in diving on these wrecks, resulting in an economic impact in the area through loss of tourism (Black et al. 2000). The weight of these mussels can also affect the structural integrity of the wrecks, causing portions to break off or collapse. Also, removing dreissnid mussels from the surfaces of these resources could result in further damage and loss (Watzin et al. 2001). A dramatic example of this is the wooden name-board on the stern quarter of the schooner *Kyle Spangler* (see Figures 30 and 31 in *Pressures* section).

In addition, when mussels colonize steel structures such as walls, pipes, and iron fasteners and fittings on shipwrecks, the iron and steel corrodes at a significantly accelerated rate as compared to ferrous material not encrusted with mussels (Watzin et al. 2001). As dreissenid colonies grow, a thick layer of organic matter accumulates under a mat of living and dead shell material, and a complex community of bacteria becomes established. These microorganisms are likely facilitating the corrosion process because they are capable of lowering pH levels on substrate surfaces, thus greatly increasing rates of corrosion (Little et al. 2000, Watzin et al. 2001). Since many of the wooden ships in the Thunder Bay sanctuary are primarily iron and steel fastened, the structural integrity of these resources could potentially be compromised (Watzin et al. 2001).

In some locations, mussels have also been shown to contribute to the concentration of toxic metals on and in the proximity of shipwrecks. A study by LaValle et al. (1999) showed that as a consequence of utilizing shipwrecks as suitable attachment substrates, the wastes from the mussels necessarily accumulate on the shipwrecks.

12. *What is the status of key species and how is it changing?*

Thunder Bay National Marine Sanctuary regulations specify the management of only maritime archaeological resources. For this reason, this question was deemed "not applicable."

13. *What is the condition or health of key species and how is it changing?*

Thunder Bay National Marine Sanctuary regulations specify the management of only maritime archaeological resources. For this reason, this question was deemed "not applicable."

14. *What are the levels of human activities that may influence living resource quality and how are they changing?*

As described in Question 11, the introduction of zebra and quagga mussels (dreissenids) in the Great Lakes has caused declines in maritime archaeological resource quality. However, the cause of this introduction (transoceanic shipping and ballast water exchange in the late 1980s) is now regulated; these regulations are in place to prevent or minimize new introductions. Therefore, although some potentially harmful activities exist that could pose a concern for invasions of new species, they do not appear to currently have a negative effect on maritime archaeological resources. For this reason, this question is rated as "good/fair" with a "not changing" trend.

The dispersal of dreissenid mussels is mediated by both natural (currents, birds and other animals) and human-related mechanisms (Carlton 1993). Human mechanisms include those related to waterways, vessels, navigation and fishery activities, and a wide variety of miscellaneous vectors (e.g., intentional movements, aquarium releases, and scientific research). The various life stages of mussels (larvae, juveniles and adults) can be transported by one or more of the following mechanisms: currents, animals, canals, ballast water, other vessel water, fish stocking, bait bucket, fire truck water, aquarium releases, amphibious planes and scientific research. Ballast water in transoceanic vessels was the initial cause of mussel introduction from Europe to the Great Lakes.

Living Resources Status & Trends

#	Issue	Rating	Basis for Judgment	Description of Findings
9	Biodiversity	N/A	Thunder Bay National Marine Sanctuary regulations specify the management of only maritime archaeological resources. For this reason, Questions 9 & 10 were deemed "not applicable."	N/A
10	Extracted Species	N/A		N/A
11	Non-indigenous Species	–	Zebra and quagga mussel colonization is causing archaeological resources to deteriorate and hinders the ability to accurately and precisely conduct archaeological documentation.	Non-indigenous species have caused or are likely to cause severe declines in maritime archaeological resources.
12	Key Species	N/A	Thunder Bay National Marine Sanctuary regulations specify the management of only maritime archaeological resources. For this reason, Questions 12 & 13 were deemed "not applicable."	N/A
13	Health of Key Species	N/A		N/A
14	Human Activities	–	The original vector for invasion is not likely to affect the future fate of existing mussels, but could introduce other non-indigenous species.	Some potentially harmful activities exist, but they do not appear to have had a negative effect on maritime archaeological resources.

Status: Good　Good/Fair　Fair　Fair/Poor　Poor　Undet.

Trends: Improving (▲), Not Changing (—), Getting Worse (▼), Undetermined Trend (?), Question not applicable (N/A)

Figures 47 and 48. Top: The scattered but well-preserved remains of the steamer *New Orleans* (1844-1849; 13-foot depth) are representative of many shallow-water shipwreck sites in and around the sanctuary. Wrecked in Thunder Bay in 1849, the 185-foot side-wheel steamer carried thousands of passengers from Buffalo to the western Great Lakes and is archaeologically significant. Bottom: A diver examines the wheel of the schooner *F. T. Barney* (1856-1868; 170-foot depth), wrecked off Rogers City, Mich. Sitting upright and intact, the site is representative of 24 similarly preserved and archaeologically significant sites in and around the sanctuary.

Photos: NOAA Thunder Bay NMS

Maritime Archaeological Resources

15. What is the integrity of known maritime archaeological resources and how is it changing?

As with any question regarding archaeology, context plays an important role in determining the answer. As indicated previously, Lake Huron's cold, fresh water ensures that Thunder Bay's shipwrecks are among the best preserved in the world, some nearly completely intact with a high degree of physical integrity. For the purposes of this report, however, the archaeological integrity of Thunder Bay's resources has been assessed irrespective of their preservation versus shipwrecks located in other environments around the world; instead, the resources have been evaluated within the context of the Great Lakes environment. It is important to note, however, that

although the state of preservation and archaeological integrity are often closely tied, a site does not have to be "intact" to be considered archaeologically significant (Figures 47 and 48). For example, the scattered but well-preserved timbers of the 1844 paddlewheel steamer *New Orleans* possess high archaeological value because few examples of such craft exist.

The response to this question is rated "good/fair" because selected archaeological resources exhibit indications of disturbance or change, but there appears to have been little or no reduction in historical, archaeological or educational value. The presence of mussels (see Question 11) is the primary reason for a "good/fair" rather than a "good" rating. Here again, context plays an important role. The presence of invasive mussels on nearly all sanctuary sites currently makes detailed data retrieval difficult — although the information still exists, it is beneath a layer of invasive mussels. As described in Question 11, it is possible that mussels are causing permanent damage, though the scale of the damage and the time over which it is occurring is not presently known. Additionally, although future negative human impacts can be lessened (and indeed, some have been; see *Response* section), the slow, natural deterioration of sanctuary resources is inevitable, though generally occurring on a timescale that is generations long rather than months or years. For this reason, the trend is considered "declining," although this too must be taken within context.

Of the 45 known shipwreck sites in the sanctuary's current 448-square-mile boundary, sanctuary staff and partners have conducted field assessments at 44 sites. Of the 47 known wrecks in the proposed expansion area, the sanctuary has conducted field assessments at 32 sites. Conducted using various methods and data, including diver observations, sonar images, physical measurements, hand drawn maps, and video and still imagery acquired by divers and remotely operate vehicles, these assessments form the basis for judging the integrity of Thunder Bay's maritime archaeological resources. The reader is directed to the *Site History*, *Pressures*, and *Response to Pressures* sections for representative visuals of sanctuary shipwreck sites and data products.

Several factors influence a shipwreck's integrity from the moment of its sinking to the present, with some factors playing more significant roles than others. Shipwreck sites addressed in this report occur in a range of locations and environments (i.e. nearshore vs. offshore, consistently cold vs. seasonally changing water temperatures, sand vs. hard bottom, etc.) and depths (0-300 feet), and represent a wide range of ship types and casualty causes. These factors and more play a role in the "site formation process," which

is essentially the cumulative effect of forces at play on a shipwreck site from its sinking to the present. In and around the sanctuary, there is substantial variation in the way archaeological sites have formed, each presenting researchers with unique opportunities.

For example, as mentioned previously, depth has a considerable impact on a site's formation. Deeper shipwrecks are generally more intact than shallower sites and have greater potential for smaller artifacts to survive in context. Conversely, shallower sites located in more dynamic environments will become broken up more easily, but may more readily reveal internal construction and design attributes difficult or impossible to document in fully intact shipwrecks. Though the sites look physically much different, each retains archaeological integrity. Notably, the resources addressed in this report break down into well-balanced depth categories: 45 sites are located at depths of 0-30 feet; 23 sites are located at depths of 31-130 feet; 18 sites are located at depths of 131-200 feet; and six sites are located at depths greater than 200 feet. Coupled with the historical significance of the vessels, the result is an impressive and comprehensive archaeological record.

In some cases, similar ship types may be studied via the dual lenses of different archaeological site formation processes. For example, the sister ships *Norman* and *Grecian*, both 300-foot-long steel bulk freighters built in 1890 and 1891, respectively, provide unique opportunities to study historically significant ship architecture. Resting in 200 feet of water, the mostly intact *Norman* retains many features not present at the shallower *Grecian* site, which rests in just 100 feet of water (Figures 49 and 50). Conversely, the *Grecian's* many exposed construction features allow for detailed study, and its shallower depth affords divers more time to work. Other steamers and schooners located in and around the sanctu-

 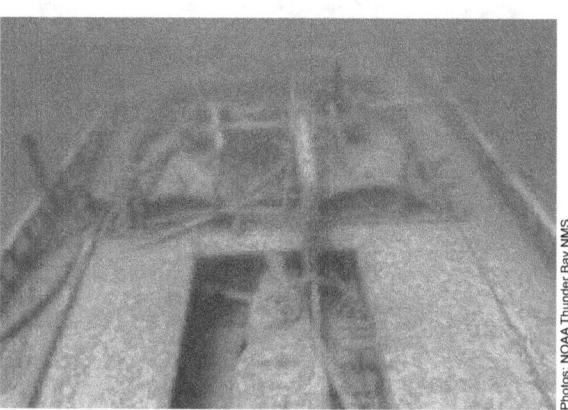

Figures 49 and 50. Left: The steamer *Norman* (1890-1895; 200-foot depth) with its boiler deckhouse, mast, nearly entire hull and many other features intact. Right: *Norman's* sister ship *Grecian* (1891-1906; 100-foot depth) in shallower water with boiler deckhouse gone, providing good access to the two boilers and many features below. In the foreground is the ship's triple expansion steam engine. The sites are very complementary, with their different depths and site formations revealing different elements of the same ship type.

ary, though not sister ships, exist at similar complementary depths.

Finally, and most powerfully, the archaeological integrity of individual sanctuary resources is strengthened tremendously by the fact that, collectively, Thunder Bay's shipwrecks present a microcosm of Great Lakes commercial shipping and culture. The area's shipwrecks reflect transitions in ship architecture and construction methods, from wooden sailboats to steel-hulled vessels, and represent virtually all types of vessels used on the open Great Lakes. These vessels were engaged in nearly every type of trade, thereby linking Thunder Bay inextricably to Great Lakes commerce. Encompassing an extensive array of historical themes, backed by an impressive archaeological record, Thunder Bay's collection of shipwrecks presents a broad history of Great Lakes culture.

16. Do known maritime archaeological resources pose an environmental hazard and how is this threat changing?

Known maritime archaeological resources within the sanctuary pose no environmental threats. One known shipwreck outside the sanctuary's eastern boundary may still contain fuel oil, but there have been no reported fuel leaks since the vessel's sinking in 1959. Therefore, this question is rated "good" with a "stable" trend.

The shipwreck within the sanctuary that historically represented the greatest environmental hazard is the German freighter *Nordmeer*, given the large quantity of fuel oil onboard when the vessel grounded just north of Thunder Bay in 1966. The removal of fuel oil is well documented and was carried out within the first five years of the vessel's sinking. A number of contractors and government agencies coordinated the removal of the vessel's fuel oil. On July 16, 1971, Michigan State Rep. Joseph P. Swallow announced that officials of the U.S. Environmental Protection Agency, in conjunction with the U.S. Coast Guard and Michigan Department of Natural Resources, made a final inspection of the sunken freighter and determined that the vessel was free of oil (*The Alpena News*, 1971). Because small amounts of oil were still trapped in the inaccessible piping system and bulkheads of the *Nordmeer*, it was postulated that an iridescent sheen of oil would continue to be visible on the surface of the water around the vessel when certain weather conditions prevail.

In 2010, a small amount of residual oil was discovered at the *Nordmeer* site, creating a light sheen on the water's surface. The U.S. Coast Guard Alpena Station and the sanctuary responded in a well-coordinated effort. The oil discovered in 2010 was determined to be residual oil located in the vessel's piping, allowed to leak to the surface when a mating flange between two pipes broke and water temperatures warmed sufficiently to make the oil less viscous. The pipe has since been capped off and no sheen has reappeared at the site.

Just outside the sanctuary's eastern boundary is the wreck of the Liberian-flagged freighter *Monrovia*. Built in 1943 in Scotland, the vessel was converted from coal to oil fuel in 1950 (Lloyd's Register of Shipping, 1950). The victim of a collision with the Canadian steamer *Royalton*, *Monrovia* sank in 1959 with no loss of life. The quantity of fuel oil onboard at the time of the vessel's sinking is not presently known, but one informal estimate made by the U.S. Coast Guard's 9th District well after the sinking, and reported in *The Alpena News*, suggested that less than 50,000 gallons would have been onboard at the time of *Monrovia*'s sinking. The sanctuary is currently conducting historical research and contacting divers and salvagers who have worked on the site (the wreck's steel cargo was salvaged) in an effort to determine if any fuel oil remains. Retired local salvager Robert Massey has related to the sanctuary that his company did not remove any fuel oil because the water was too cold and the oil too viscous (R. Massey, pers. comm., 2012). To date, the sanctuary is not aware of any current or historic reports of fuel leaking from the wreck site. Should the question remain unresolved through historical research, the sanctuary will work with appropriate partners to investigate the wreck of *Monrovia* and determine its potential as an environmental hazard.

Additional 20th-century shipwrecks occur in and around the sanctuary, including *Viator* (1904-1935), *D. R. Hanna* (1906-1919), *W. H. Gilbert* (1892-1914), *W. C. Franz* (1901-1934), *Etruria* (1902-1905) and *Isaac M. Scott* (1909-1913). The sanctuary has determined that none of these shipwrecks carried fuel oil.

Notably, should sanctuary expansion occur, the proposed boundaries would include a 1,300 square-mile area that has potential for unexploded ordnance and military-related debris within it. NOAA's Lake Huron chart 14860 contains a note cautioning mariners against "anchoring, dredging, or trawling in the area due to the possible existence of unexploded ordnance." As demonstrated by recent University of Michigan (U of M) research, the potential for prehistoric archaeological sites exists in this area. The sanctuary partnered with U of M in 2010 to map the area with multibeam sonar and again in 2011 to ground truth promising targets with divers. Given the potential for both prehistoric and historic archaeological resources, as well as the area's significance as a fish habitat, the sanctuary is interested in facilitating a fuller cultural and natural assessment of the area. The sanctuary is currently working with the Michigan Department of Environmental Quality (MDEQ) Superfund Section to identify stakeholders with an interest in assessing the area. MDEQ has requested assistance from the U.S. Army Corps of Engineers to evaluate the known munitions in the area (Figures 51 and 52) and potentially address their findings via the Military Munitions Response Program.

17. What are the levels of human activities that may influence maritime archaeological resource quality and how are they changing?

The various human activities identified in the "*Pressures on Sanctuary Resources*" section of this report can have measurable impacts to maritime archaeological resources, but evidence suggests effects are localized, not widespread. For this reason, this question is rated as "fair" with an "improving" trend.

Visiting dive boats and divers have the greatest potential to influence the quality of maritime archaeological resources. This includes anchor damage to sites, leaving temporary mooring lines attached to sites where the lines later become derelict, poor diving practices by divers (e.g., brushing mussels off delicate wood surfaces or handling and moving artifacts), and souvenir hunting and looting. The sanctuary's shipwreck mooring program, education and outreach efforts, and enforcement efforts in partnership with the U.S. Coast Guard mitigate some of these pressures at selected sites. However, the prevalence and degree of these kinds of disturbances at all sites in and around the sanctuary is not known.

Consistently monitoring sites particularly susceptible to diver impacts is an important first step, but this evidence must be correlated with overall diving activity in the sanctuary to be truly meaningful. Currently, the sanctuary does not have a precise accounting of diving activity in and around the sanctuary, although it maintains good relationships with area dive charter businesses. Informal data suggests that there is a significant demand for scuba diving charter services in the Thunder Bay area, with two of the most established dive charter businesses reporting nearly full capacity over the last two years. Currently, four dive charter businesses are located in Alpena and Rogers City. Several southern Michigan and out-of-state charters also visit sanctuary resources. Additionally, there are private vessels that visit sanctuary resources.

At present, it is unknown if there are more or fewer dive boats and divers visiting the sanctuary in comparison to previous years. Per the sanctuary's 2009 Final Management Plan, the sanctuary is developing a mechanism whereby dive charters and private vessels visiting the sanctuary can voluntarily submit diving statistics. The sanctuary is currently (2012) working with the University of Michigan's Economic Development Administration University Center to study the broader economic and cultural impacts of the sanctuary on the region. Included in this study is a mechanism to measure the number of divers and dive charters visiting the sanctuary.

Maritime Archaeological Resources Status & Trends

#	Issue	Rating	Basis for Judgment	Description of Findings
15	Integrity	▼	Mussel colonization and natural deterioration will persist, but resulting declines in integrity are slow. Management actions have slowed diver and boating impacts.	Selected archaeological resources exhibit indications of disturbance, but there appears to have been little or no reduction in historical, scientific, or educational value.
16	Threat to Environment	—	Few, if any, wrecks pose an environmental threat, and those that do are localized.	Known maritime archaeological resources pose few or no environmental threats.
17	Human Activities	▲	All human activities are on the decline due to management actions (e.g., mooring, education, and enforcement activities).	Selected activities have resulted in measurable impacts to maritime archaeological resources, but evidence suggests effects are localized, not widespread.

Status: Good Good/Fair Fair Fair/Poor Poor Undet.

Trends: Improving (▲), Not Changing (—), Getting Worse (▼), Undetermined Trend (?), Question not applicable (N/A)

Photos: University of Michigan Anthropology Department

Figures 51 and 52. Top: An object tentatively identified as a military munitions (Zuni unguided rocket) was discovered by University of Michigan researchers in an area being proposed for sanctuary expansion. Bottom: Modern debris exists in the area, as well. With various partners, the sanctuary is helping to facilitate an assessment of the area.

Response to Pressures

This section describes responses to pressures outlined earlier in this document, including specific research, education and outreach activities aimed at protecting sanctuary resources. Responses are based on the sanctuary's management plan that was released in 2009 (TBNMS 2009), as well as initiatives undertaken since that time. The management plan is the result of more than two years of study, planning, and extensive public input and addresses key issues and opportunities affecting the sanctuary.[10]

Research and Characterization: A Foundation for Responding to Pressures

Research and characterization form the foundation of the sanctuary's resource protection efforts, and underpin responses to specific pressures. Characterization is the process through which resources are located, inventoried, assessed and ultimately analyzed within a broader historical, archaeological and resource management context. Characterization makes informed resource protection possible because it widens the view for resource managers, allowing research efforts to be prioritized and balanced against staff, budget and operational realities.

Characterization is accomplished through a variety of research methods. From archival research to remote sensing and individual site assessment and documentation, research forms the foundation for responding to pressures on sanctuary resources. Archaeological and historical research is also at the heart of the sanctuary's exhibits, education initiatives and public programming, all of which is designed to foster greater awareness and appreciation for the Great Lakes and their rich maritime history. Notably, much of the sanctuary's research is made possible with grants and other outside funding — since 2005, the sanctuary has obtained more than $435,000 from external sources for on-water research and resource protection, greatly supplementing its core resource protection budget.

Thunder Bay Sanctuary Research Collection

Characterization of the sanctuary and its resources begins with an inventory of known and potential maritime archaeological resources in the region. The inventory is based on archival research of contemporary newspapers, lifesaving station and ship logs, vessel enrollments, insurance and court records, and other published and unpublished literature.

Much of this research is conducted in the Thunder Bay Sanctuary Research Collection, itself an important sanctuary resource requiring preservation and management efforts. Managed jointly by the sanctuary and the Alpena County George M. Fletcher Public Library, the Thunder Bay Research Collection is a large and unique archival collection dedicated to Great Lakes maritime history. The heart of the collection was amassed over more than 40 years by historian C. Patrick Labadie. Labadie and his wife June Perry contributed the collection to the sanctuary in 2003. Since that donation, dozens of other donors have fortified the collection, and a partnership with the University of Wisconsin-Superior's Jim Dan Hill Library has enhanced the collection's 20th-century holdings.

The collection now includes more than 1,000 published works, 80,000 photographs, 56 linear feet of vertical files, 40 feet of periodicals, 100 navigation charts, 350 shipbuilding plans, various manuscripts, and files on more than 20,000 Great Lakes watercraft. The collection also contains information on Great Lakes ports, cargos, ship owners and captains, ship technology, and archaeology. Because it is a significant sanctuary resource and open to the public, a major focus has been to digitize the collection. A $235,000 grant from the Michigan Department of History, Arts, and Libraries, nearly $160,000 from the NOAA Climate Database Modernization Program and hundreds of volunteer hours made possible the creation of an online database of 17,000 vessels and related photographs. Digitization accelerates the pace of historic research, fosters greater public access to the collection, and aids in the preservation of fragile documents by reducing the need for direct physical handling (TBNMS 2009).

Locating Maritime Archaeological Resources

Physically locating maritime archaeological sites is the next step in sanctuary characterization and resource protection. Remote sensing surveys have been undertaken within the sanctuary and surrounding waters with assistance from NOAA, universities and other partners. As of 2011, 361 square miles have been surveyed within the sanctuary's current 448-square-mile boundary. An additional 246 square miles have been surveyed outside the sanctuary's boundaries. Since designation, the sanctuary has discovered and identified

---

[10] See http:// hunderbay.noaa.gov/management/mpr for the sanctuary's Final Management Plan (FMP) and related documents. The FMP will be referenced throughout the Response section of this Condition Report. Beyond research and resource protection, the plan also outlines strategies and ac ivities relevant to sanctuary education, outreach and operations.

Partners in Preservation

The sanctuary relies heavily on the work of others to help respond to pressures on its resources. Many groups and individuals impart energy, expertise, and equipment critical to sanctuary resource protection. Leveraging these partnerships is critical to the sanctuary's successful and sustained management of its resources. Still other partners have their own research objectives, aimed at both cultural and natural resources, and the sanctuary actively supports these efforts.

A research partner's presence in Alpena also has an important effect on the local economy, further strengthening the sanctuary's tie to the community. In 2011, 98 individuals spent 278 overnight stays in the Alpena area in support of sanctuary-related work.

Sanctuary research partners include:

- Cooperative Institute for Ocean Exploration, Research and Technology
- Dr. Robert Ballard's Institute for Exploration
- East Carolina University, Program in Maritime Studies
- East Carolina University, Diving and Water Safety Program
- Grand Valley State University, Annis Water Resources Institute
- Great Lakes Naval Memorial and Museum
- Michigan Department of Environmental Quality
- Michigan Department of National Resources
- Michigan Underwater Preserve System
- National Association of Black Scuba Divers
- NOAA, Great Lakes Environmental Research Laboratory
- NOAA, National Geodetic Survey, Remote Sensing Division
- NOAA, National Undersea Research Center
- NOAA, Office of Coast Survey, Navigation Response Team
- Noble Odyssey Foundation

- PAST Foundation
- University of Connecticut, Marine Sciences Program
- University of Michigan, Anthropology Department
- University of Michigan, Geomicrobiology Lab
- University of Michigan, Marine Hydrodynamics Lab
- University of Michigan, Naval Architecture and Marine Engineering
- University of Michigan, Perceptual Robotics Lab
- University of North Carolina, Coastal Studies Institute
- University of Rhode Island, Joint Program in History/Archaeological Oceanography
- University of Texas at Austin, Applied Research Lab
- University of Vermont, The Rubenstein School of Environment and Natural Resources
- University of Wisconsin-Stout, Biology Department
- U.S. Naval Sea Cadets-Great Lakes Division
- U.S. Coast Guard-Alpena Station
- Woods Hole Oceanographic Institution

five intact shipwreck sites at depths between 160 and 300 feet, as well as hundreds of targets in shallow water representing the scattered remains of an undetermined number of shipwrecks and other historic features such as pound net stakes, pilings and cribs.

A major side-scan sonar survey covering approximately 240 of the sanctuary's 448 square miles was undertaken in 2001 (the year following sanctuary designation) by Robert Ballard's Institute for Exploration. The team confirmed the locations of 15 sites in and around the sanctuary, produced the sanctuary's first sonar images of these sites, and discovered the wreck of the schooner *Corsican* (1862-1893; 160-foot depth) and a submerged sinkhole in 300 feet of water. Significantly, the effort covered nearly half of the sanctu-

Figures 53 and 54. Two separate remote sensing efforts in 2010 resulted in the discovery of one new shipwreck and an enhanced understanding of a submerged land bridge that runs across Lake Huron. The darker area (left) represents sonar data acquired with a forward-looking sonar mounted on a REMUS 600 autonomous underwater vehicle (right). The 52-hour survey covered 104 square miles at an average rate of two square miles per hour. The colored area in the image on the left is multibeam data acquired using the sanctuary's R/V Storm. Logging 52 hours of survey time, the team mapped 46 square miles.

ary's area, primarily offshore, allowing future remote sensing efforts to focus on relatively easier to survey nearshore areas.

In partnership with the University of Rhode Island, and bolstered with funding from NOAA's Office of Ocean Exploration and Research, three seasons of side-scan sonar surveys have resulted in an additional 109 square miles of coverage both within and beyond the sanctuary's boundaries. The team discovered the wreck of the steamer *Messenger* (1866-1890; 190-foot depth) in 2008. Earlier efforts, conducted as graduate-level field schools, focused on the shallow waters around Thunder Bay Island, Sugar Island and North Point Reef, resulting in more than 200 targets of interest in a three-square-mile area.

NOAA Office of Ocean Exploration and Research grant funding has been instrumental in making possible two other major surveys. In 2010, a team from the sanctuary and the University of Michigan's Anthropology Department set out to search for prehistoric archaeological sites along the Alpena-Amberley Ridge. Around 7,500 years ago, this now-submerged land bridge spanned northern Lake Huron, connecting Michigan and Canada. Working 50 miles offshore with a multibeam sonar temporarily installed on the sanctuary's R/V Storm, the team mapped 46 square miles of lake bottom. The effort allowed University of Michigan anthropologists to model a portion of the land bridge and make better predictions as to where prehistoric people may have lived and hunted, which in turn has focused subsequent research. Additionally, in 2010, the sanctuary and the Applied Research Lab at University of Texas-Austin surveyed 104 square miles in and around the sanctuary. Using forward-looking sonar developed by the Applied Research Lab mounted on a REMUS 600 autonomous underwater vehicle, the

team discovered the wreck of the steamer *Egyptian* (1873-1897; 240-foot depth), as well as other targets of interest in shallower water (Figures 53 and 54).

In 2011, the sanctuary added to its remote sensing infrastructure a RESON 8101 multibeam sonar, surplused from NOAA's Office of the Coast Survey. Now installed permanently on the R/V *Storm*, the sonar was used in 2011 to survey 70 square miles off Presque Isle, Mich. Much of the surveying took place during the Sony- and Intel-funded Project Shiphunt, which brought five Saginaw, Mich., high school students to the sanctuary to search for a historic wreck and work alongside researchers from NOAA and the Woods Hole Oceanographic Institution. The team discovered the wrecks of the *Etruria* (1902-1905; 300 foot-depth) and schooner *M. F. Merrick* (1863-1889; 300-foot depth).

An important by-product of sonar surveys designed to locate shipwrecks is the production of bathymetry and maps that can be used by scientists interested in the sanctuary's natural resources. Although not all sonar data is useful for this purpose, the sanctuary is acquiring an ever-increasing amount of this data type. For example, in partnership with the sanctuary, NOAA's Office of the Coast Survey has been surveying with multibeam and side-scan sonar much of Thunder Bay proper, producing approximately 40 square miles of highly detailed bathymetry maps as of 2011. The project's aim is to map the entirety of Thunder Bay and the waters south of Sugar and Thunder Bay Islands by 2013 (Figure 55). The effort was undertaken primarily to update NOAA nautical charts for the area, but it has also proven effective at producing the first detailed bathymetric maps of Thunder Bay. As it becomes available, the data is shared with researchers at the Michigan Department of Natural

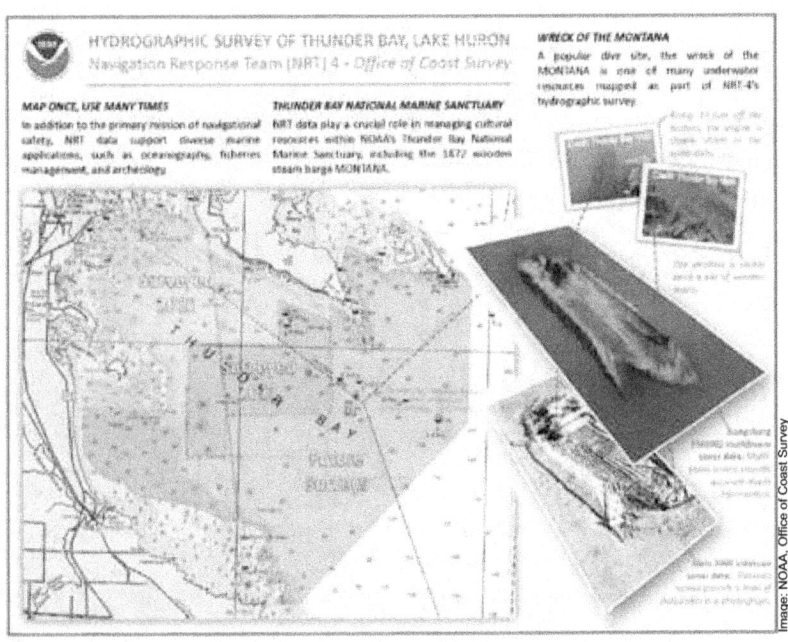

Figure 55. Working with other NOAA offices helps the sanctuary acquire data useful for sanctuary resource management. The data is also shared with a variety of scientists and institutions interested in the natural and ecological aspects of Thunder Bay.

Resources and the Environment, U.S. Fish and Wildlife Service, U.S. Geological Survey, and NOAA Great Lakes Environmental Research Lab, all of which are conducting research and monitoring in Thunder Bay. Additionally, the data helped scientists plan fieldwork for the 2012 Lake Huron Coordinated Sampling Initiative, much of which focused on Thunder Bay.[11]

The sanctuary has also facilitated the use of other types of remote sensing technology. In 2006, leveraging assets from NOAA's Remote Sensing Division, the sanctuary used aerial-borne topographic LIDAR (Light Detection and Ranging) to map the shoreline around Thunder Bay, and also produced high-resolution photogrammetry to about the 18-foot depth contour. Similar to radar but using light pulses instead of radio waves, LIDAR is typically "flown" or collected from planes and produces a rapid collection of points (more than 70,000 per second) over a large collection area, with resolution to about one meter. The

project was successful in that the locations of several shallow-water shipwreck sites were confirmed via photogrammetry. Information such as this helps bridge the gap between marine and terrestrial environments, and is useful for shoreline communities as they seek better data to assist with planning. The data also establishes a baseline for comparing historical and archival information on the dynamic maritime landscape of the city of Alpena over time, which includes changes to the waterfront and fluctuations in commercial structures.

Supplementing high-tech acoustic remote sensing surveys, particularly in shallow water, are visual surveys done by divers or even topside from a shallow-draft research vessel. Surveys of this type have been especially productive on North Point Reef, where nearly 70 vessels stranded since the middle of the 19th century. Although the majority of vessels were ultimately recovered, about a dozen remain on the reef. A visual survey in 2004 by sanctuary staff recorded more than several dozen targets on the reef. In 2005, a team of graduate students from East Carolina University's (ECU) Program in Maritime Studies focused on creating a site plan for wreckage thought to belong to the propeller *Galena* (1857-1872; 16-foot depth), stranded on the reef in 1872. *Galena* was lost not far from the propeller *Congress* (1861-1868; 17-foot depth) and the steam barge *B.W. Blanchard* (1870-1904; nine-foot depth), as well as the schooners *John T. Johnson* (1873-1904; seven-foot depth), *Empire State* (1862-1877; 12-foot depth) and *E.B. Palmer* (1856-1892; 16-foot depth). Wreckage from some or all of these vessels was located during the visual survey in 2004 and re-examined during the ECU field school. In total, 41 sites consisting of large sections or clusters of wreckage, anchors, rudders, windlasses and even a lifeboat davit were recorded with basic measurements, scaled drawings and photographs.[12] These targets,

---

[11] The Coordinated Science and Monitoring Initiative is a bi-national effort between Canada and the U.S. to jointly address the top science and monitoring priorities for the Great Lakes on an individual lake level. Each year, on a rotating five-year basis, one Great Lake receives enhanced bi-national monitoring support, resources and attention — the so-called "Year of Coordinated Monitoring." For 2012, the chosen lake is Lake Huron, with an additional (and first-time) focus on Thunder Bay. Priorities are identified by the Lakewide Management Plan management committees, and coordinated through a bi-national steering committee.

[12] Notably, much of the research and an analysis of North Point provided content for an ECU student's master's thesis (see Pecoraro 2007).

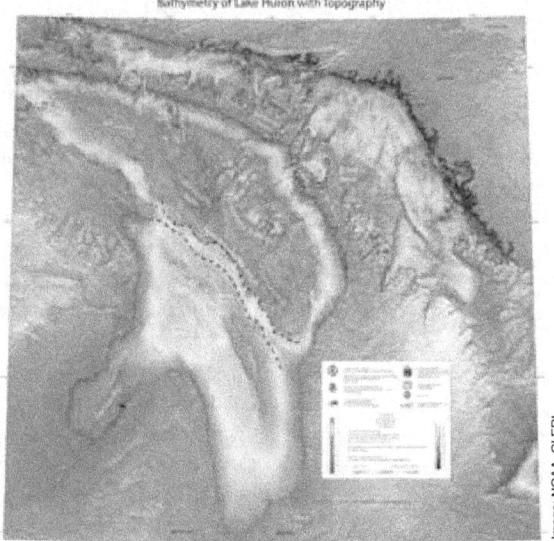

Bathymetry of Lake Huron with Topography

Image: NOAA, GLERL

Figure 56. A bathymetry map of Lake Huron showing the Alpena-Amberley Ridge, which once connected Michigan with Canada. University of Michigan anthropologists are searching the area for prehistoric archaeological sites.

as well as those obtained during other visual and acoustic surveys are prioritized, managed and stored in the sanctuary's geographic information system.

Additionally, new research by the University of Michigan aims to determine the archaeological potential of the Alpena-Amberley Ridge (Figure 56), a now-submerged land bridge that once connected Michigan with Canada. Roughly 9,900 – 7,500 years ago, the ridge formed a dry land corridor extending across Lake Huron from Presque Isle in northeast Michigan to the Point Clark area in southern Ontario. This land bridge would have provided a natural causeway for the migration of caribou and valuable terrain for hunters seeking to exploit the herd. Pilot research by the University of Michigan's Department of Anthropology suggests that stone features potentially used by Arctic caribou hunters are preserved on the ridge and can be recognized using acoustic mapping. In 2010, the sanctuary assisted with mapping 44 square miles of the ridge, identifying significant targets and generating enough bathymetry data to produce a dynamic 3D model. In 2011, the team made 61 dives to "ground truth" many of the sonar targets.

Finally, in 2012, the Noble Odyssey Foundation, a longtime sanctuary partner, continued visually surveying prehistoric drowned forest remains from a range of depths in the Thunder Bay area. With assistance from U.S. Naval Sea Cadet divers, the team expanded its understanding of an area discovered in 2010 through the discovery of additional tree stumps 22 feet below the present lake level.

The R/V *Storm* and NOAA's Green Fleet in the Great Lakes

Much of Thunder Bay sanctuary's research is accomplished with the use of the R/V Storm. *Originally built in 1992 as a United States Coast Guard prototype, the* Storm *served in Baltimore, Md., and later at the U.S. Merchant Marine Academy in Long Island, N.Y. Acquired on surplus and extensively refitted in 2009 by the NOAA Great Lakes Environmental Research Lab (GLERL), the 50-foot vessel is another "Green Ship" in NOAA's Great Lakes fleet.*

The Storm's *B100 fuel is produced from soy bean oil and reduces emissions by more than 70 percent. Engine oil, lubricants and hydraulic oils are manufactured from a variety of vegetable oils. These biomaterials are sustainable and far less toxic than conventional petroleum oils. The focal point of the* Storm's *green attributes is its low rebuild carbon footprint. Through careful engineering and creative use of recycled materials, the 18-year-old vessel was rebuilt to add value and extend its useful life. For its "Green Ship" innovations, GLERL has been awarded the U.S. Department of Energy's "You Have the Power" Award.*

Radiocarbon dating by the University of Arizona reveals that the stumps at this depth contour are 7,000-8,000 years old. The ages of wood from different depths in Thunder Bay will indicate how fast lake levels were rising during that period. Equally significant is the potential for prehistoric cultural material to be located along these ancient shorelines.

Site Assessment and Documentation

Once archaeological sites are located, they are assessed and documented. Site location, integrity and depth generally dictate the methodology and equipment with which a site is assessed and later documented archaeologically. Assessments provide baseline data to evaluate a site's current state of preservation and plan and prioritize future documentation and permanent mooring installations. It also allows for the initial identification of threats to sites, such as invasive mussel coverage, natural deterioration, anchor damage, looting and other impacts. Sanctuary staff have conducted field assessments at 44 of the 45 known shipwreck sites within the sanctuary's current 448-square-mile boundary. Of the 47 known wrecks in the proposed expansion area (see *Site History* and *Going Forward: Sanctuary Boundary Expansion sections*), the sanctuary has conducted field assessments at 32 sites. Assessments are conducted using various methods and data, including diver observations, sonar images, video and still imagery acquired by remotely operate vehicles (Figure 57).

Detailed archaeological documentation is generally conducted with trained divers manually mapping wreck sites. Divers can be sanctuary staff, university and other partners, or volunteers. Many partners and volunteers have had sanctuary-sponsored training in archaeological methods (see *Education and Outreach* section). In 2011, the sanctuary and its partners made more than 350 dives in support of sanctuary research and resource protection projects. Using manual mapping techniques, the sanctuary and its partners have produced archaeological site maps for 24 shipwrecks in and around the sanctuary (Figures 58 and 59). The maps capture a site's state of preservation, establish baseline data from which to monitor and

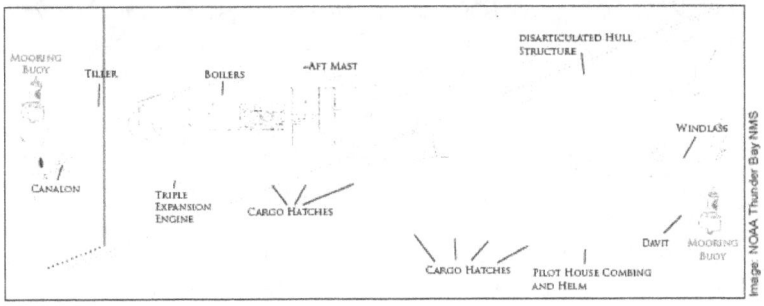

Figure 57, 58, and 59. Left: Site assessments are conducted using a variety of data, from sonar images to direct observation by divers. This side-scan sonar image of the schooner *M. F. Merrick* (discovered by the sanctuary in 2011) is a good example and offers much useful data. At 300 feet deep, the wreck's assessment relied chiefly on this image, which in turn informed follow-up ROV and SCUBA dives to the site.

Top Right: A sanctuary archaeologist uses manual mapping methods to document a shipwreck. These methods are used to produce site maps like the one above of the steamer *Grecian* (1891-1906; 90-foot depth). This 300-foot-long bulk freighter is one of the sanctuary's most popular shipwrecks and represents an important link between wooden and steel shipbuilding techniques. Data like this provides a baseline assessment from which to monitor future changes at the site. To increase public accessibility and prevent anchor damage, the site is marked with a sanctuary mooring buoy.

Figures 60 and 61. Top Left: A perspective drawing of the schooner *Defiance*, resting in 185 feet of water outside the sanctuary's northern boundary. Many popular, intact shipwrecks lay in deeper waters outside the sanctuary. In an effort to better understand and protect these impressive time capsules, the sanctuary and its partners regularly work outside the sanctuary. Top Right: NOAA archaeologists take measurements of the *Defiance* in order to produce a detailed map of the wreck site.

manage future impacts to the site, provide archaeological data to researchers, and serve as the basis for a number of outreach products. This type of documentation has occurred at popular shipwreck sites such as the *Grecian* (1891-1906; 100-foot depth), *E. B. Allen* (1864-1871; 100-foot depth), *New Orleans* (1838-1849; 13-foot depth), *Shamrock* (1875-1905; 11-foot depth), and *Monohansett* (1872-1907; 18-foot depth), as well as other shallow-water shipwreck sites near North Point, Whitefish Point, Isaacson Bay, Forty-Mile Point and Black River.

Given the popularity of technical diving (using specialized equipment to dive deeper than 130 feet) and the human pressures that can be exerted on the exceptional resources at these depths, the sanctuary and its partners are increasingly assessing and documenting shipwrecks at depths between 130 and 300 feet (Figures 60 and 61). Many of these sites are located outside the sanctuary's current boundaries and possess significant preservation and archaeological integrity (see *Site History and Resources* section). In 2001, Robert Ballard's Institute for Exploration laid the groundwork by obtaining high-definition video at many of these sites with remotely operated vehicles (ROVs), *Little Hercules* and *Argus*. The University of Michigan's *M-Rover* has also been used to capture dozens of hours of

video. Since 2005, sanctuary archaeologists have used mixed-gas diving and decompression techniques to access these complex sites.

Using a variety of data, assessments have been conducted at 17 shipwrecks in technical depth ranges, including popular sites such as the *John J. Audubon* (1854-1854; 170-foot depth), *Florida* (1889-1897; 200-foot depth), *New Orleans* (1885-1906; 130-foot depth), *Norman* (1890-1895; 220-foot depth), *Typo* (1873-1899; 160-foot depth), *F. T. Barney* (1856-1868; 160-foot depth), and *Monrovia* (1943-1959; 140-foot depth). With the help of partners, assessments have also occurred at the recently discovered sites *Egyptian* (1873-1897; 240-foot depth), *Etruria* (1902-1905; 310-foot depth), *M. F. Merrick* (1863-1889; 300-foot depth) and *Messenger* (1866-1890; 195-foot depth). More detailed documentation has occurred at the *Corsican* (1862-1893; 160-foot depth), *Defiance* (1848-1854; 185-foot depth), *Kyle Spangler* (1856-1860; 185-foot depth) and *Pewabic* (1863-1865; 160-foot depth). The assessment of deepwater shipwrecks is significantly enhanced by contributions from skilled volunteer technical divers willing to contribute their video, still images and site observations.

Notably, the sanctuary is also an excellent training ground for students studying maritime history and archaeology, and those efforts contribute to the sanctuary's ability to document maritime ar-

Toward a Better Understanding of Thunder Bay

Although sanctuary regulations pertain only to maritime archaeological resources, the sanctuary is dedicated to facilitating scientific research and monitoring that improves our understanding of Lake Huron's natural resources. Beyond data sharing, such as bathymetry maps produced during sanctuary remote sensing operations, the sanctuary regularly provides scientific diving, research vessel, housing, lab support and workspace for a variety of multidisciplinary projects.

Reef Restoration

Since 2008, the sanctuary has provided planning, logistical, diving and research vessel support for the Thunder Bay Reef Restoration project, coordinated by the Michigan Department of Environmental Quality. Nearly 1.5 acres of new reef habitat have been created along the eastern shores of Alpena, with the goal of mitigating the loss of natural reef habitat from previous decades of cement kiln dust disposal. A total of 29 individual reefs have been placed near two existing natural reefs. The project is made possible by a grant from the Estuary Restoration Act (NOAA) Estuary Habitat Restoration Program in conjunction with the United States Army Corps of Engineers and the donation of more than 13,000 tons of limestone cobble by Lafarge – Alpena Plant.

A Thunder Bay NMS diver places an egg collection net on an experimental reef in Thunder Bay.

A Window into Earth's Past

In an ongoing effort to support and facilitate multidisciplinary research at the Middle Island submerged sinkhole, the sanctuary's research team regularly conducts scientific dives for researchers from Grand Valley State University's Microbial Biology Lab, the University of Michigan's Geomicrobiology Lab, the University of Wisconsin-Stout, and NOAA's Great Lakes Environmental Lab as they continue to characterize the specialized ecosystem present at the Middle Island sinkhole. At this sinkhole location, colorful microbial mats with bubbling gasses have been discovered which are not found anywhere else in the Great Lakes, and are known to occur in just a few other places on Earth (Biddanda et. al 2012). Recent genetic research suggests that the sinkhole's modern bacteria are 2.5 billion-year-old cousins to some of Earth's first oxygen-using organisms.

A Thunder Bay NMS diver prepares to take a sediment core at the Middle Island Sinkhole. The work by TBNMS divers supports research by Grand Valley State University and the University of Michigan"

Keeping an Eye on the Weather

In 2004, the Thunder Bay sanctuary and NOAA's Great Lakes Environmental Research Lab (GLERL) placed an Integrated Coastal Observing System buoy in the sanctuary at the shipwreck Montana, nine miles from shore. The buoy is equipped with a host of sensors that provide real-time meteorological data, such as air temperature, wave height and direction, wind speed and direction, and temperatures throughout the water column. The sanctuary and GLERL also mounted a meteorological station at the entrance to the Thunder Bay River. This station provides real-time weather data and has a camera that continuously generates three real-time views of Thunder Bay. Both observing systems are used regularly by commercial and recreational boaters in Thunder Bay.

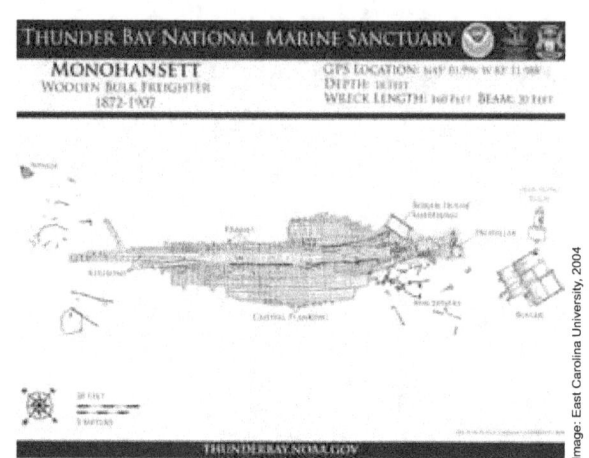
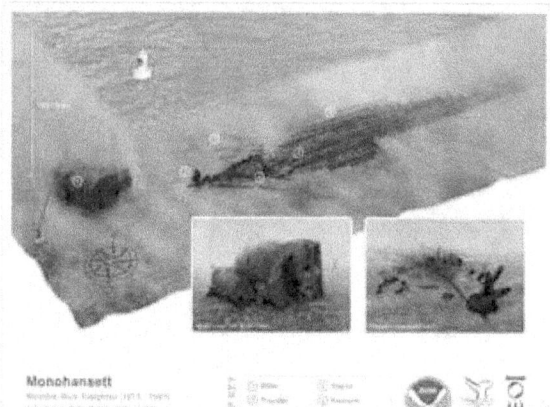

Figures 62 and 63. Left: A shipwreck site plan of the steamer *Monohansett* produced by graduate students in East Carolina University's Program in Maritime Studies. With living quarters, classroom space and easy access to shipwrecks, the Great Lakes Maritime Heritage Center is an excellent venue for field schools and avocational training in maritime archaeology. Products produced during these projects benefit the students, the sanctuary and the public. Right: A rendering of the *Monhansett* site made possible by the archaeological site plan. Available online, the map is available to divers, snorkelers, kayakers and glass bottom boat passengers who visit the popular, shallow-water site.

chaeological sites (Figures 62 and 63). The sanctuary has hosted field schools for students from East Carolina University, University of Rhode Island and University of Michigan.

Specific Responses to Pressures: Diving and Looting

The sanctuary encourages public access to its resources and strives to balance increased visitation with resource protection. The following outlines management responses to the pressures on sanctuary resources that were outlined earlier in this report.

Shipwreck Moorings

As indicated earlier in this report, there are photographic evidence and diver reports of disturbance at sanctuary shipwreck sites due to human activities. Both divers, as well as dive boats, can negatively impact sanctuary resources. To eliminate anchor damage to shipwrecks sites, the sanctuary installs and maintains a growing number of permanent moorings at popular sites (Figures 64-66). The first system was installed in 2003. Currently, 27 sites are marked with U.S. Coast Guard-approved moorings, and the sanctuary has approved permits for 30 new sites. Moorings also eliminate the need for non-permitted moorings at shipwreck sites, which can become derelict over time, posing a risk to divers and potentially damaging the site. Finally, moorings encourage public accessibility and make

for safer diving by providing a sturdy means of descent and ascent for divers, and an easy-to-find surface marker for kayakers. Mooring buoys are installed and recovered seasonally to avoid ice and storm damage during winter months. Moorings are typically available from May 15 through Oct. 1, but weather can occasionally delay seasonal redeployments. The sanctuary's website provides divers with the up-to-date status of each mooring. Sanctuary regulations prohibit the use of grappling hooks or other anchoring devices on maritime archaeological resource sites if a mooring buoy is available at the site (TBNMS 2009).

Education and Outreach

Ultimately, resource protection is a shared responsibility between the sanctuary and a wide range of stakeholders. At the front lines of this effort are divers who visit sanctuary sites directly. Fostering appreciation for sanctuary resources among divers is fundamental to reducing human impacts at these unique, irreplaceable sites. Divers, and other stakeholders, will protect what they value. Through focused education and outreach the sanctuary strives to articulate the message that the shipwrecks of Thunder Bay are historical, archaeological and recreational sites worth protecting. The sanctuary conducts substantial education and outreach activities designed to reach multiple audiences including educators, students, tourists and the local community, among others.[13]

---

[13] In 2011, the sanctuary's Great Lakes Maritime Heritage Center welcomed over 73,000 visitors. Tailored programs aimed at K-12 students reached approximately 2,700 local students, while additional specialized programming for all ages and interties reached an addi ional 6,800. Learn more about the sanctuary's education programs in he 2009 Final Management Plan and www.thunderbay.noaa.gov/education.

Although divers benefit from all of the sanctuary outreach efforts, this section of the report identifies efforts directed chiefly at divers, with the express purpose of fostering a preservation ethic.

National and regional diving trade shows, maritime archaeological workshops and academic symposiums are important venues to meet with divers. These provide opportunities to discuss concerns in the dive community, reinforce the benefit of responsible diving through presentations and outreach literature, and build partnerships. Since 2004, sanctuary archaeologists have staffed informational booths and given presentations at many regional and national venues, including *Gales of November* (Duluth, Minn.), *Dive into the Past* (Minneapolis/St. Paul, Minn.), *Ghost Ships Festival* (Milwaukee, Wisc.), *Our World Underwater* (Chicago, Ill.), *Great Lakes Shipwreck Festival* (Ann Arbor, Mich.), *Boston Sea Rovers* (Boston, Mass.), and the *Society for Historical Archaeology Annual Conference* (various national locations). Sanctuary staff attend several of these events annually. In 2011, sanctuary archaeologists gave presentations and staffed informational booths at three major Midwest diving trade shows with an overall attendance of over 11,000.

Reaching a wider diving audience is also important, as the sanctuary seeks to deliver its preservation message via larger outlets and promote diving and tourism in the region. Since 2004, the sanctuary has facilitated and been featured in a number of television and film projects aimed at both diving and general audiences. These include: History Channel (*Deep Sea Detectives: Great Lakes Ghost Ship*), Jean-Michel Cousteau's Ocean Futures Society (*America's Underwater Treasures*), National Geographic Channel (*Drain the Great Lakes*), Radical Media/Current TV (*Project Shiphunt*), Discovery Channel Canada (*Daily Planet*), the Science Channel (*Great Lakes Shipwrecks*), and public television (*Tragedies in the Mist*).

Creating an increased sense of value toward sanctuary resources requires providing meaningful products that both facilitate public access and reinforce responsible diving. Consequently, many of the sanctuary's research products are repurposed as outreach material specifically for divers. For example, 17 of the sanctuary's archaeological site maps can be downloaded and printed via the sanctuary's website, and several have been rendered as computer animations and 2D graphics for dive planning (Figures 67 and 68). Divers can access these on the sanctuary's

website, where they will also find coordinates, images and diving-related information on 69 shipwrecks in and around the sanctuary.

Involving divers directly in the documentation of shipwreck sites helps foster a preservation ethic, while also expanding the sanctuary's research abilities. Using the Nautical Archaeology Society's curriculum

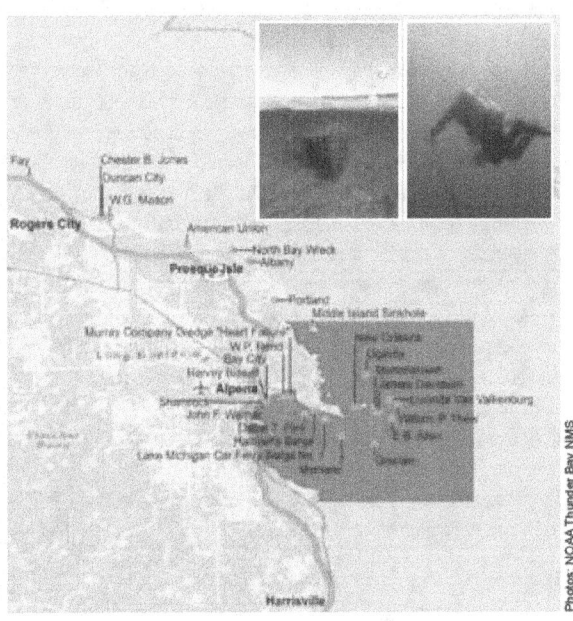

Figures 64-66. Left: locations of permanent moorings in Thunder Bay National Marine Sanctuary. Center: A sanctuary-sponsored mooring at the wreck of the steamer *Monohansett*, resting in 18 feet of water. Right: A diver ascends from a deeper dive via the safety of a sturdy mooring line.

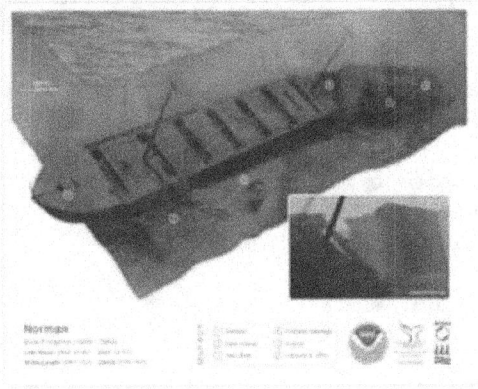
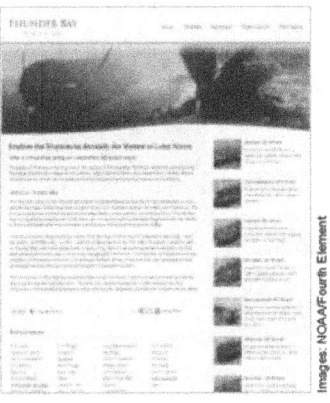

Figures 67 and 68. In 2010, sanctuary archaeologists evaluated the wreck of the Steamer *Norman* (1890-1895), resting in 200 feet of water outside the sanctuary's northern boundary. Using field data from that project and original builders plans, sanctuary partner Fourth Element created a printable 2D graphic (left) and an online interactive model (right) to help divers better plan their visit to the site. Six other shipwrecks have received a similar treatment and can be viewed online at http://thunderbaywrecks.com and http://thunderbay.noaa.gov.

and certification, the sanctuary has trained 69 divers in archaeological field methods.[14] During this hands-on archaeological training experience, students learn about historic preservation, maritime archaeological law and sanctuary-specific resource protection efforts. These "citizen scientists" include local residents, as well as members of the Michigan Underwater Preserve Council, Michigan State Police, U.S. Naval Sea Cadets and National Association of Black SCUBA Divers (Figure 69).

Similarly, in recent years the sanctuary has actively developed partnerships with skilled volunteer technical divers, a subset of the diving population that uses advanced diving methods to access the Thunder Bay region's many intact deepwater shipwrecks. This effort has led to much greater sanctuary exposure within the technical diving community, which in turn advances its resource protection efforts. This was demonstrated in 2011 after the sanctuary's discovery of the schooner *Merrick* and steamer *Etruria*, both in approximately 300 feet of water. Located in May during a Sony-funded survey, only limited ROV footage could be obtained due to a short operational and funding window. Just two months later, the sanctuary acquired excellent video and still images of the sites due to the work of skilled volunteers.[15] The effort substantially increased the time frame in which the sanctuary can assess the wrecks and plan future documentation (Figures 70 and 71). Additionally, a joint 2008 project between the sanctuary and local technical divers produced high-quality data on the wreck of the *Kyle Spangler*, which made possible the public release of its location (Figures 72 and 73).

Law Enforcement

Preventing artifact looting and other negative human impacts to sanctuary resources requires enforcement of sanctuary regulations and state laws, and a sufficient on-water presence within the sanctuary. To accomplish this, the sanctuary partners with local, state and federal law enforcement agencies including NOAA's Office of Law Enforcement, the U.S. Coast Guard (USCG), Michigan Department of Natural Resources and the Environment (MDNRE), Alpena County Sheriff, and Michigan State Police.

In 2011, the USCG Alpena-Station was underway 94 times and logged over 260 hours in and around the sanctuary, including operating at least 15 days near Presque Isle, Mich., an area under study for potential sanctuary expansion and a popular marina for dive boats. Also, the USCG Auxiliary was underway 10 times in the area, operating four times out of Presque Isle. Additionally, a USCG cutter operated in Thunder Bay proper conducting law enforcement operations for one week. This on-water presence constitutes a significant piece of law enforcement for the sanctuary.

---

[14] See http://www.nauticalarchaeologysociety.org/training

[15] Project participants were John Janzen, John Scoles, Sue Smith and Tracey Xelowski.

Figure 69. Volunteer divers contribute much to the sanctuary's ability to document shipwreck sites. Above, U.S. Naval Sea Cadets receive instruction on land before diving to record an historic shipwreck. In 2011, the Sea Cadets made more than 350 dives in the sanctuary.

Figures 70 and 71. These excellent photos of the *M. F. Merrick* taken in 2011 by volunteers significantly enhanced the sanctuary's assessment of this newly discovered shipwreck. Top: The image of the vessel's stern gives a good indication of site integrity and reveals some distinctive architectural elements, as well as coverage of invasive quagga mussels. Bottom: The vessel's cargo hold revealed substantial artifacts, including several wheelbarrows used by the crew to handle the *Merrick*'s bulk cargo. Note the presence of mussels, even inside the vessel.

The Great Lakes Maritime Heritage Center

Figures 74 and 75. NOAA's Great Lakes Maritime Heritage Center (GLMHC), in Alpena, Michigan is the sanctuary's headquarters and visitor center.

In 2005, Thunder Bay National Marine Sanctuary opened the Great Lakes Maritime Heritage Center (GLMHC), which houses the sanctuary's headquarters, research station and visitor center (Figures 74 and 75). The center provides an opportunity for the sanctuary to enhance public awareness, understanding and stewardship of the sanctuary, the Great Lakes and the ocean. The main components of the 9,000-square-foot exhibit space include a full-size replica schooner and shipwreck, along with a shipwreck gallery, artifact storage and conservation laboratory, visible curatorial space, distance-learning equipped classroom, a researchers' field station, and a 93-seat theater. The center welcomed over 73,000 visitors in 2011. Beyond education, the GLMHC serves as the anchor for heritage tourism in the region and has attracted new businesses, such as a glass bottom boat, clear-bottom kayak rentals and a dive shop, all located in the city of Alpena. Through a partnership with the University of Michigan's Institute for Research on Labor, Employment, and the Economy, the sanctuary seeks to quantify the economic impacts of these new activities starting 2012.

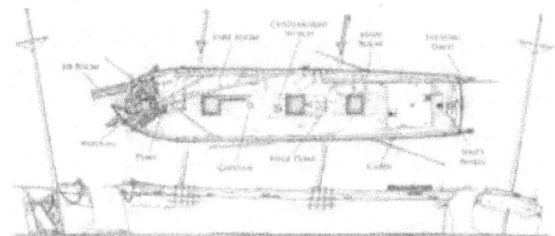 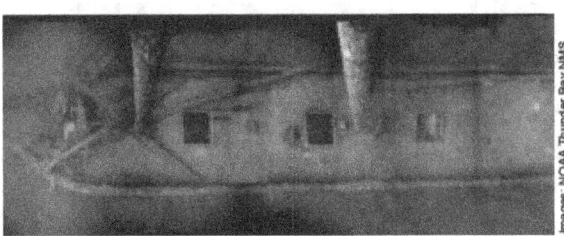

Figures 72 and 73. An archaeological site plan (left) and photomosaic (right) of the schooner *Kyle Spangler* resting in 185 feet of water off Presque Isle, Mich. The site possesses high recreational and archaeological potential, and has become a popular scuba diving attraction since its location was made known to the public in 2008. Discovered in 2003 by local diver Stan Stock, the wreck's location remained secret until the site was documented by Stock, Tracey Xelowski and sanctuary archaeologists, after which it was jointly decided to release the coordinates to the public.

The following activities are prohibited in the sanctuary without a permit:

- *Recovering, altering, destroying, or possessing underwater cultural resources.*

- *Drilling into, dredging, or otherwise altering the lake bottom associated with underwater cultural resources.*

- *Using grappling hooks or other anchoring devices if a mooring buoy exists.*

For complete regulations, see 15 C.F.R. Part 922, Subpart R. Also available online at www. thunderbay.noaa. gov/pdfs/tbnmsregs.pdf.

Figures 76 and 77. The sanctuary's conservation lab ensures that artifacts long ago removed from wrecks get appropriate treatment. Many artifacts eventually go on display in the Great Lakes Maritime Heritage Center's visible artifact storage room. Windows between the main exhibit and the conservation lab allow the public to see the restoration in real-time.

The sanctuary is also developing "interpretive enforcement" practices, which seek to enhance compliance primarily through education. The goal of interpretive enforcement is to gain the greatest level of compliance through public understanding and support of sanctuary goals. Interpretive enforcement emphasizes informing the public through education and outreach about responsible behavior before resources are adversely impacted. Law enforcement officers interact with users on the water and at the dock. These encounters allow officers to make direct, informative contacts with visitors and local residents, while conducting routine enforcement activities. Per its 2009 Management Plan, the sanctuary is developing ways to make interpretive enforcement more effective, including regular meetings with the USCG-Alpena Station and its auxiliary unit.

Facilitating continuing education for local law enforcement officials is an important aspect of sanctuary law enforcement. In 2005, the sanctuary hosted a maritime heritage law enforcement workshop for regional agencies, bringing experts from NOAA's Office of Law Enforcement to Alpena, Mich. In 2006, the sanctuary superintendent and four members of the USCG-Alpena Station and MDNRE attended a submerged cultural resources law enforcement class sponsored by Biscayne National Park. Additionally, maritime heritage law is a key component of the sanctuary's Nautical Archaeology Society training. During these classes, students learn the basics in shipwreck-specific legislation and how it applies to the sanctuary. Members of the Michigan State Police have attended this training. In Alpena in 2009, the NOAA Maritime Heritage Program sponsored a workshop on federal heritage law. The workshop focused on the National Historic Preservation Act's Section 106, which provides a process to ensure that federal activities are reviewed for potential impacts on state lands, in this case submerged bottomlands of the national marine sanctuaries. Attendees included maritime heritage coordinators and other personnel from NOAA's Office of National Marine Sanctuaries.

Coordination and communication among the several agencies involved in sanctuary law enforcement is critical. In the spring of 2006, the sanctuary established the Thunder Bay Law Enforcement Task Force to better coordinate enforcement efforts in the sanctuary. The task force focuses on improving public education and providing additional on-water and dockside patrols of the sanctuary. NOAA and the MDNRE are developing a Joint Enforcement Agreement that will further enable the MDNRE to conduct dedicated enforcement activities in the sanctuary.

Artifact Conservation

Sanctuary regulations and Michigan law prohibit the recovery of shipwreck artifacts without a permit, however, the state provides a mechanism for previously recovered artifacts to return to public ownership. In addition to protecting maritime archaeological resources submerged beneath Lake Huron's cold fresh water, the sanctuary and the Michigan Department of Natural Resources manage artifacts removed from Michigan's historic shipwrecks. Previously housed in a Lansing storage facility, the collection of more than 1,000 objects now resides at the Great Lakes Maritime Heritage Center.

The Great Lakes Maritime Heritage Center features a well-equipped conservation lab in which recovered maritime archaeological artifacts of all sizes and conditions are stabilized for long-term preservation, storage, and display (Figures 76 and 77). The sanctuary also receives artifact donations from private collections throughout Alpena and northeast Michigan. Accepted artifacts are accessioned into the state of Michigan's archaeological collection and assessed for conservation needs. Many artifacts immediately go on public display in the visible storage room at the sanctuary's Great Lakes Maritime Heritage Center. Artifacts awaiting conservation, rotation into sanctuary exhibits, or loan to other institutions are housed in a dedicated 400-square-foot storage facility.

Specific Responses to Pressures: Fishing and Boating

Recreational fishing and boating in general poses little threat to sanctuary resources, save for the snagging of tackle in shipwrecks sites during trolling. As previously mentioned, sanctuary moorings alert recreational fishermen and boaters to the presence of wrecks below. Additionally, the coordinates of all known sanctuary shipwrecks are available to the public via the sanctuary's website. Fishing is not prohibited on or around sanctuary shipwreck sites, though when divers are on site and displaying proper "diver down" signal flags other boaters must observe the proper regulations for staying clear of the area.

Although a formal study has not been done, gill net remnants are known to exist at a small number of shipwreck sites in the sanctuary. However, the potential for future impacts are not great given the limited amount of commercial fishing in the area. In addition, Native American and commercial fishermen avoid known wreck sites, as they are hazards to expensive nets.

Specific Responses to Pressures: Non-indigenous Species

The sanctuary's understanding of non-indigenous species, primarily invasive mussels, is informed chiefly by broader Great Lakes-wide efforts, many of which involve NOAA. These broader efforts are summarized below, followed by the sanctuary's role in more localized studies.

Managing the impact of harmful invasive species is a major challenge and demands a comprehensive approach involving collaboration with multiple agencies and programs across the Great Lakes region (Great Lakes Commission 2007, USEPA and Environment Canada 2009). In the 1990s the Great Lakes Fishery Commission, a bi-national partnership between the U.S. and Canada, was tasked with developing guidelines for ballast water management to help prevent the spread of zebra mussels. Also in 1990, Congress passed the Nonindigenous Aquatic Nuisance Prevention and Control Act, which was prompted largely by the damage caused by the introduction and spread of zebra mussels. A task force was formed, which allowed for a strong state, tribal, nongovernmental, federal, and bi-national partnership. The task force is co-chaired by representatives of the U.S. Fish and Wildlife Service and NOAA. It is responsible for the following actions (Great Lakes Commission 2007):

- Public education — Specific user groups are targeted via out-

reach methods such as watercraft inspection, regulation booklets, waterfront signage and advertising for recreational boaters.

- Policy, regulations and enforcement — Mechanisms are being created to ensure compliance with prevention and control measures (e.g., prohibition of the possession, sale or transport of live aquatic invasive species).

- Early detection, monitoring and rapid response — Innovative management strategies enhance the capacity to anticipate, prevent and respond to new aquatic invasions before they become established.

- Predictive modeling — Use of life history analysis and computer modeling helps to identify potential new invaders and forecast their possible range of infestation.

In 2007, Canada implemented mandatory ballast water control and management regulations for both ballast and No Ballast on Board vessels. The U.S. has instituted mandatory ballast water requirements for ballast vessels and voluntary management guidelines for No Ballast on Board vessels. (Great Lakes Commission 2007)

The Great Ships Initiative is an innovative collaboration among multiple private, state and federal agencies whose objective is to resolve the problem of ship-mediated invasive species in the Great Lakes-St. Lawrence Seaway System through independent research and demonstration of environmental technology, financial incentives, and consistent basin-wide harbor monitoring. The near-term objective of the initiative is to significantly accelerate research, development and implementation of effective ballast treatment systems for ships that visit the Great Lakes from overseas. The initiative includes numerous stakeholders at the federal, state and academic level, including NOAA (Cangelosi and Mays 2006).

There are also various public education and outreach campaigns being implemented at the local, state, regional and national levels to prevent and slow the spread of non-indigenous species. *Stop Aquatic Hitchhikers!* is a national campaign established by the U.S. Fish and Wildlife Service in conjunction with the task force and the U.S. Coast Guard designed to educate recreational water resource users on non-indigenous species and provide advice on voluntary guidelines for prevention and control. *Habitattitude* is a national campaign implemented jointly by the Pet Industry Joint Advisory Council, the U.S. Fish and Wildlife Service, and the NOAA National Sea Grant College Program. It targets aquarists and water gardeners in order to prevent the release of unwanted aquarium plants and fish (Great Lakes Commission 2007).

Regionally, the sanctuary is working to develop and support partnerships with multi-disciplinary researchers and organizations to study Great Lakes ecology including the study of invasive species. From

2008 to 2010, the sanctuary research team conducted a series of dives in Saginaw Bay to support mussel sampling efforts by NOAA's Great Lakes Environmental Lab (GLERL) and several partner organizations. Begun in 2007, the five-year project is studying the complex multiple stressors impacting the Saginaw Bay ecosystem. The research is being used to develop, evaluate and operationalize GLERL's Adaptive Integrated Framework, using Saginaw Bay as a blueprint that can be applied at other coastal systems facing similar stressors and management issues. Partners include the University of Michigan, Michigan State University, University of Akron, Limno-Tech, Western Michigan University, Michigan Department of Natural Resources, and Michigan Department of Environmental Quality. Sampling by sanctuary divers provides data critical to the project's invasive mussel component.

In 2012, as part of GLERL's Long-Term Ecological Research program, the mussel sampling model used and refined in Saginaw Bay will be implemented in Thunder Bay. This effort coincides with the broader Lake Huron Coordinated Science and Monitoring Initiative (CSMI), which has a significant Thunder Bay component in 2012.[16] Among other research objectives, the CSMI aims to understand the impact of invasive species in Thunder Bay. The sanctuary supports the CSMI and its many partners by providing divers, research vessels, lab space and living quarters. Notably, the 2012 GLERL and CSMI efforts represent a significant milestone in the study of the Thunder Bay ecosystem, and one that is occurring in part because of the sanctuary's presence in Alpena. Supplementing ongoing research by the Michigan DNRE, U.S. Fish and Wildlife Service and U.S. Geological Survey, the CSMI effort represents the first step in a longer-term process of coordinated Lake Huron monitoring by multiple agencies.

Specific Responses to Pressures: Natural Deterioration

Unlike human impacts, the natural deterioration of shipwrecks is difficult or impossible to curb on a large scale. However, it is possible in selective cases to intervene in a way that stalls the inevitable effects of time. The *S. P. Ely* Project in Lake Superior is a good example of reinforcing a ship's hull to prevent an impending collapse.[17] In this case, the integrity of this shallow-water site (and appeal to divers) was extended by at least a decade.

The primary way the sanctuary responds to the natural deterioration of sanctuary resources is through documentation (see *Site Assessment and Documentation* section). This is typically the first step in any program of scientific analysis of how chemical, biological and physical processes may be affecting sanctuary resources. Documentation captures a site's current state of preservation and integrity, thereby creating a permanent record. Documentation can sometimes help mangers and archaeologists identify natural degradation causes, but most significantly, it serves as a baseline from which to monitor those impacts into the future. Of the 45 known shipwreck sites in the sanctuary's current 448-square-mile boundary sanctuary staff have conducted field assessments at 44 sites. Of the 47 additional known wrecks in the proposed expansion area, sanctuary staff have conducted field assessments at 32 sites. The sanctuary also encourages divers to donate images of shipwrecks, which significantly expands both the sanctuary's and the public's understanding of these important sites, and accelerates research and monitoring. Conducting assessments and gaining a baseline understanding of all sites within the sanctuary, and many beyond the current boundaries, have been a primary focus of the sanctuary's research to date. A logical next step for sanctuary resource protection efforts is the implementation of a meaningful and sustainable monitoring program.

The effects of climate change on Lake Huron and sanctuary resources are a significant avenue of potential research for the sanctuary and its partners. To that end, the sanctuary encourages, facilitates and actively participates in research projects that seek to understand and monitor environmental changes in Lake Huron. In 2012, for example, the EPA-led Lake Huron Bi-national Partnership conducted an intensive monitoring program on Lake Huron (Cooperative Science and Monitoring Initiative) (EPA 2008). The sanctuary provided sanctuary-acquired bathymetric data, research vessels, staff and working space at the sanctuary's Great Lakes Maritime Heritage Center. Data from this and similar efforts will inform future Thunder Bay National Marine Sanctuary condition reports.

Going Forward: Sanctuary Boundary Expansion

To provide protection for unique historic sites within Michigan's northern Lake Huron maritime landscape, but beyond the current boundaries of Thunder Bay National Marine Sanctuary, NOAA is evaluating the possible expansion of the sanctuary's boundaries. The genesis of the proposed expansion can be found in the sanctuary's Final Management Plan (2009), in which a working group consisting chiefly of members of the Thunder Bay National Marine Sanctuary Advisory Council recommended that the sanctuary expand its boundaries to protect shipwrecks and other maritime heritage resources in waters adjacent to the current sanctuary. The advisory

---

[16] The CSMI is a bi-national effort between Canada and the U.S. to jointly address the top science and monitoring priorities for the Great Lakes on an individual lake level. Priorities are identified by he Lakewide Management Plan management committees and coordinated through a bi-national CSMI Steering Committee.

[17] See Merryman 1995

council determined that expanding sanctuary boundaries will help protect important national historic sites through the sanctuary's well-established research, resource protection (including law enforcement), and education programs, while allowing recreational use of the resources. Moreover, within the new boundary is the potential for the discovery of several dozen more shipwrecks, as well as related archeological sites such as docks, cribs, piers and prehistoric sites.

Based on the working group's recommendation, supporting research by sanctuary staff, and strong public support and comment during public meetings, the sanctuary has identified a study area that encompasses 4,300-square-miles, including all of Alcona, Alpena and Presque Isle counties, selected submerged maritime heritage resources in Cheboygan and Mackinaw counties, and extending offshore to the Canadian border. Expanding the boundaries in this way would add 47 known shipwrecks to the sanctuary. Among them are some of the Great Lakes' best-preserved and most recreationally significant shipwrecks. Archival research indicates that as many as 64 shipwrecks are yet to be discovered in this expanded area. Adding this new area to the sanctuary would result in a 4,300-square-mile sanctuary containing 92 known historic shipwrecks and the potential to discover as many as 100 additional sites.

The study area was chosen after considering the several boundary alternatives put forth during the sanctuary's original designation (2000), as well as expansion alternatives later developed by the sanctuary advisory council (2007), and finally after receiving considerable public input during public scoping meetings (2012). At the time of this condition report's publication, the sanctuary is writing a draft environmental impact statement, which will be available for public comment. The document describes in detail the three different boundary alternatives being considered (Figure 78), and the environmental and socioeconomic impacts of expansion. A description of the boundary expansion process and related documents can be found at: www.thunderbay.noaa.gov/management/mpr/boundary.com

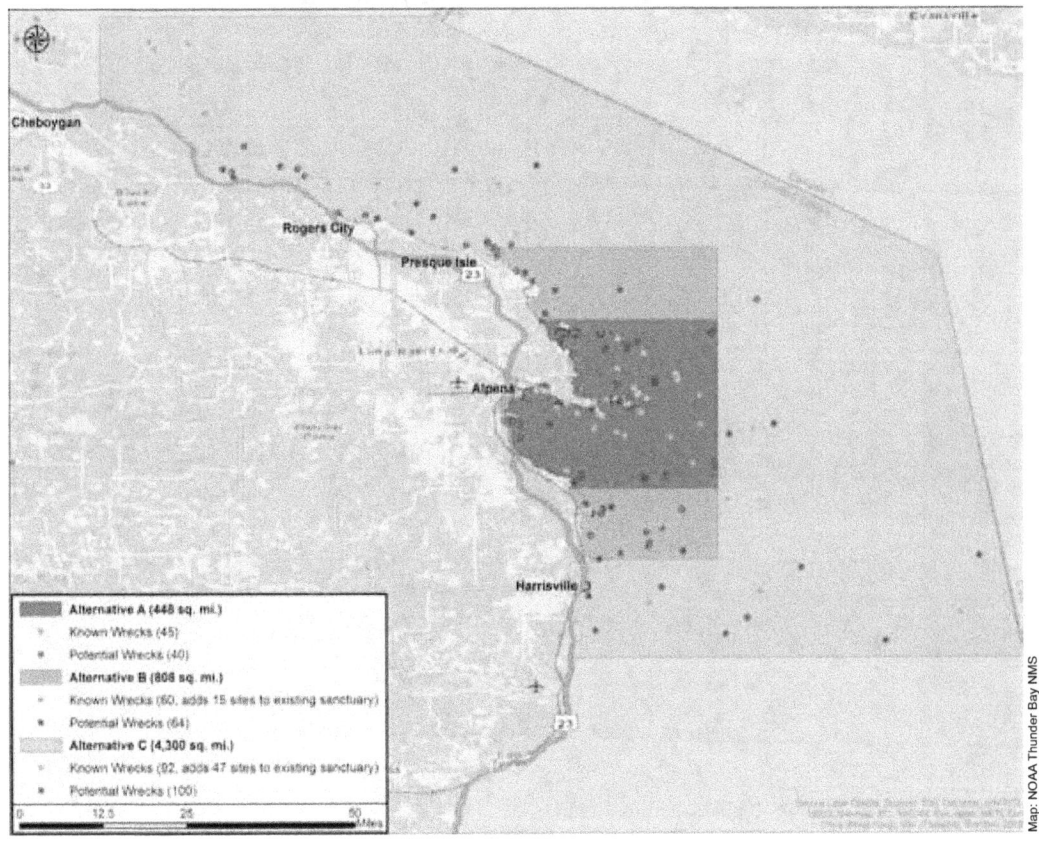

Figure 78. TBNMS Boundary Expansion Options. Green dots represent known shipwrecks, red dots are potential shipwrecks (locations based on historical records). Potential boundary alternatives are indicated by color: Dark blue = Alternative A; medium blue = Alternative B; light blue = Alternative C.

Acknowledgements

The staff of Thunder Bay National Marine Sanctuary would like to acknowledge the assistance and efforts of subject area experts from the NOAA Great Lakes Environmental Research Laboratory (GLERL), who, by participating in a workshop in March 2010, provided responses to questions that guided the drafting of the "State of Sanctuary Resources" section of this report: Doran Mason, Tom Nalepa, Steve Ruberg, Ed Rutherford and Craig Stow.

The report benefited significantly from the following individuals who either provided a preliminary review of the report or provided comments, content, images, and/or data:

Ellen Brody (ONMS Northeast Region), Tane Casserley (TBNMS), Karen Fox (formerly of TetraTech), Jeff Gray (TBNMS), Joe Hoyt (MNMS), John Jensen (Maritime Studies and Policy Faculty, Sea Education Association), Matthew Lawrence (SBNMS), Jennifer Lukens (NOAA Office of Habitat Restoration), Wayne Lusardi (Michigan State Underwater Archaeologist), Sarah Opfer (NOAA Marine Debris Program), David Reid (GLERL), Mitchell Tartt (ONMS), and Hans Van Tilberg (NOAA Maritime Heritage Program).

Finally, our sincere thanks are extended to the peer reviewers of this document: Frank Cantelas (NOAA Office of Ocean Exploration and Research), James Johnson (Michigan Department of Natural Resources), and Steve Kroll (Great Lakes Divers).

Cited Resources

Abbott, G.M., J.H. Landsberg, A.R. Reich, K.A. Steidinger, S. Ketchen, C. Blackmore. 2009. Resource guide for public health response to harmful algal blooms in Florida. Fish and Wildlife Research Institute Technical Report TR-14. viii + 132 p.

Argyle, R.L. 1991. Status of forage fish stocks in Lake Huron 1990. Report on file at the National Fisheries Research Center – Great Lakes, Ann Arbor, Mich.

Assel, R.A. 2003. An electronic atlas of Great Lakes ice cover. NOAA Great Lakes Ice Atlas, Great Lakes Environmental Research Laboratory, Ann Arbor, Mich. Electronic document available from: http://www.glerl.noaa.gov/data/ice/atlas/

Assel, R.A. 2005. Great Lakes weekly ice cover statistics. NOAA Technical Memorandum GLERL-133. NOAA Great Lakes Environmental Research Laboratory, Ann Arbor, Mich.

Bially, A. and H.J. MacIsaac. 2000. Fouling mussels (*Dreissena* spp.) colonize soft sediments in Lake Erie and facilitate benthic invertebrates. Freshwater Biology 43:85–97.

Biddanda, B.A., S.C. Nold, G.J. Dick, S.T. Kendall, J.H. Vail, S.A. Ruthberg, C.M. Green. 2012. Rock, water, microbes: underwater sinkholes in Lake Huron are habitats for ancient microbial life. Nature Education Knowledge 3(3):13.

Black, M.G., D.F. Reid, S.J. Nichols, S. Hautau, G.W. Kennedy. 2000. Impacts of zebra mussel infestations on the shipwrecks of Thunder Bay, Lake Huron. Diving for Science in the 21st Century. 16pp.

Bootsma, H.A., E.B.Young, J.A.Berges, 2004. *Cladophora* research and management in the Great Lakes. Proceedings of workshop, December 2004: Special Report No. 2005-01. UWM Great Lakes WATER Institute.

Boulton, W. 1884. History of Alpena County. *In:* Michigan Pioneer and Historical Collections. W.S. George and Company, Lansing, Mich.

Brewer, R., G.A. McPeek, R.J. Adams , Jr. 1991. The atlas of breeding birds of Michigan. Michigan State University Press, East Lansing, Mich.

Cangelosi, A. and N. Mays. 2006. Great ships for the Great Lakes? Commercial vessels free of invasive species in the Great Lakes-St. Lawrence seaway system. Northeast Midwest Institute. 145pp. Electronic document available from: http://www.nemw.org/images/stories/documents/scopingreport.pdf

Carlton, J.T. 1993. Dispersal mechanisms of the zebra mussel (*Dreissena polymorpha*). *In*: Zebra mussels: biology, impacts, and control. Lewis Publishers, Boca Raton, FL. pp. 677-697. NOAA Oregon Sea Grant No. R/EM-19.

Carr, M.H. and M.A. Hixon. 1997. Artificial reefs: the importance of comparisons with natural reefs. Special Issue on Artificial Reef Management, Fisheries 22(4):28-3.

Connelly, N.A., C.R. O'Neill, B.A. Knuth, T.L. Brown. 2007. Economic impacts of zebra mussels on drinking water treatment and electric power generation facilities. Environmental Management 40: 105–112.

Doermann, L. 2012. Great Lakes geologic sunken treasure: submerged sinkholes in Lake Huron offer a look back to ancient Earth. Earth Magazine. August 2012. Electronic document available from: http://www.earthmagazine.org/article/great-lakes-geologic-sunken-treasure

EPA (Environmental Protection Agency). 2008. Lake Huron bi-national partnership, 2008-2010 action plan. 90pp. Electronic document available from: http://epa.gov/greatlakes/lamp/lh_2008/index.html

Fielder, D. G., J. S. Schaeffer, and M. V. Thomas. 2007. Environmental and ecological conditions surrounding the production of large year classes of walleye (*Sander vitreus*) in Saginaw Bay, Lake Huron. J. Great Lakes Res. 33(sp1):118-132.

Fourqurean, J.W., J.N. Boyer, M.J. Durako, L.N. Hefty, B.J. Peterson. 2003. Forecasting Response of Seagrass Distributions to Changing Water Quality Using Monitoring Data. Ecological Applications 13(2)474-489.

Franks Taylor, R., A. Derosier, K. Dinse, P. Doran, D. Ewert, K. Hall, M. Herbert, M. Khoury, D. Kraus, A. Lapenna, G. Mayne, D. Pearsall, J. Read, B. Schroeder. 2010. The sweetwater sea: an international biodiversity conservation strategy for Lake Huron – technical report. A joint publication of The Nature Conservancy, Environment Canada, Ontario Ministry of Natural Resources Michigan Department of Natural Resources and Environment, Michigan Natural Features Inventory Michigan Sea Grant, and The Nature Conservancy of Canada. 264 pp. with Appendices.

GLERL (NOAA Great Lakes Environmental Research Laboratory). 2008. Zebra and quagga mussel research at NOAA's Great Lakes Environmental Research Laboratory. Electronic document available from: http://www.glerl.noaa.gov/pubs/brochures/20ZMresearch.pdf

Great Lakes Commission. 1992. Counterattack: Great Lakes panel targets aquatic nuisance species. Electronic document available from: http://www.glc.org/ans/counterattack.html

Great Lakes Commission. 2007. Great Lakes Aquatic Invaders. 7pp. Electronic document available from: http://www.glc.org/ans/aquatic-invasions

Gonzalez, M.J. and A. Downing. 1999. Mechanisms underlying amphipod responses to zebra mussel (*Dreissena polymorpha*) invasion and implications for fish-amphipod interactions. Can. J. Fish. Aquat. Sci. 56:679–685.

Goode, G.B. 1887. The fisheries and fishing industries of the United States. Government Printing Office, Washington, D.C.

Halpern, B.S., K.A. Selkoe, F. Micheli, C.V. Kappel. 2007. Evaluating and ranking the vulnerability of global marine ecosystems to anthropogenic threats. Conservation Biology 21(5):1301-1315.

Haltiner, R.E. 1986. The town that wouldn't die: a photographic history of Alpena, Michigan from its beginnings through 1940. Village Press Inc., Traverse City, Mich.

Haltiner, R.E. 2002. Stories the red people have told and more: a testimonial to N.E. Michigan's "long-ago-people.", Model Printing, Alpena, Mich.

Harding, J.H. and J.A. Holman. 1990. Michigan turtles and lizards: a field guide and pocket reference. Mich. State Univ. Cooperat. Ext. Serv., East Lansing, Mich.

Harvell, C.D., K. Kim, J.M. Burkholder, R.R. Colwell, P.R. Epstein, D.J. Grimes, E.E. Hofmann, E.K. Lipp, A.D.M.E. Osterhaus, R.M. Overstreet, J.W. Porter, G.W. Smith, G.R. Vasta. 1999. Emerging marine diseases - climate links and anthropogenic factors. Marine Ecology 285:1505-1510.

Hecky, R.E., R.E.H. Smith, D.R. Barton, S.J. Guildford, W.D. Taylor , M.N. Charlton, and T. Howell. 2004. The nearshore phosphorus shunt: a consequence of ecosystem engineering by dreissenids in the Laurentian Great Lakes. Canadian Journal of Fisheries Aquatic Sciences 61: 1285-1293.

Herdendorf, C.E., S.M. Hartley, M.D. Barnes. 1980. Fish and wildlife resources of the Great Lakes coastal wetlands within the United States. USFWS FWS/OBS-81/02-V4. U.S. Fish and Wildlife Service, Washington, D.C.

Higgins, S.N. and M.J. Vander Zanden. 2010. What a difference a species makes: a meta-analysis of dreissenid mussel impacts on freshwater ecosystems. Ecological Monographs 80:179–196.

International Joint Commission Canada and the United States. 2001. 15th Biennial report on Great Lakes water quality, January 2001. Electronic document available from: http://www.ijc.org/rel/boards/watershed/15biennial_report_web-final.pdf.

Johnson, J. 2010. Changes in Lake Huron's ecosystem and food web cause Chinook salmon collapse. Michigan Department Natural Resources, Fisheries Report.

Kraft, C. 1996. Zebra mussel update #26: The great cover up. University of Wisconsin-Madison, Wisconsin SeaGrant Institute.

LaValle, P.D., A. Brooks, V.C. Lakhan. 1999. Zebra mussel wastes and concentrations of heavy metals on shipwrecks in western Lake Erie. J. Great Lakes Res. 25(2):330-338.

Lindquist, D.G., I.E. Clavijo, L.B. Cahoon, S.K. Bolden, S.W. Burk. 1989. Quantitative diver visual surveys of inner shelf natural and artificial reefs in Onslow Bay, NC: Preliminary results for 1988 and 1989, p. 219:227. *In*: M.A. Lang and W.C. Jaap (eds.) Diving for Science 1989. American Academy of Underwater Sciences, Costa Mesa, Calif.

Little, B.J., R.I. Ray, R.K. Pope. 2000. Relationship between corrosion and the biological sulfur cycle: a review. Corrosion 56(4):433-443.

Lloyd's Register of British and Foreign Shipping 1950/51 Steamers & Motorships. Lloyds Register of Shipping. Register Book. Register of Ships 1950/51.

Lusardi, W.R. 2011. Rock, paper, shipwreck! The maritime cultural landscape of Thunder Bay. *In*: B. Ford (ed.), The Archaeology of Maritime Landscapes, When the Land Meets the Sea 2, pp. 81-97, Springer Science+Business Media.

Merryman, K. 1995. S.P. Ely Restoration Project Report. Electronic document available from: http://www.glsps.org/ely.htm

MSG (Michigan Sea Grant). 2009a. Zebra mussel fact sheet.

MSG (Michigan Sea Grant). 2009b. Quagga mussel fact sheet.

Nalepa, T.F., D.L. Fanslow, S.A. Pothoven, A.J. Foley, G.A. Lang. 2007. Long-term trends in benthic macroinvertebrate populations in Lake Huron over the past four decades. J. Great Lakes Res. 33:421-436. Electronic document available from: http://www.glerl.noaa.gov/pubs/fulltext/2007/20070020.pdf

NMSP (National Marine Sanctuary Program). 2004. A monitoring framework for the National Marine Sanctuary System. U.S. Dept. of Commerce, National Oceanic and Atmospheric Administration, National Ocean Service. Silver Spring, MD. 22 pp. Electronic document available from: http://sanctuaries.noaa.gov/library/national/swim04.pdf

NOAA (National Oceanic and Atmospheric Administration). 1999. Thunder Bay National Marine Sanctuary Final Environmental Impact Statement/Management Plan. A Federal/State Partnership for the Management of Underwater Cultural Resources. Office of Ocean and Coastal Resource Management. 335pp. Electronic document available from: http://thunderbay.noaa.gov/pdfs/thunderbayeis.pdf

NPS (National Park Service). 1997. Cultural Resource Management Guideline, Release No. 5, (NPS-28), 179 pp.

ONMS (Office of National Marine Sanctuaries). 2009. Environmental Assessment for the Final Management Plan. 12pp. Electronic document available from: http://thunderbay.noaa.gov/pdfs/ea.pdf

Pecoraro, T.A. 2007 Great Lakes ship traps and salvage: a regional analysis of an archaeological phenomenon. Master's Thesis, Department of History, East Carolina University, Greenville, N.C.

Pennak, R.W. 1989. Fresh-water invertebrates of the United States: Protozoa to Mollusca. John Wiley & Sons, Inc., N.Y.

Quimby, G.I. 1960. Indian life in the Upper Great Lakes. University of Chicago Press, Chicago, Ill.

Riley, S. C., E. F. Roseman, S. J. Nichols, T. P. O'Brien, C. S. Kiley, and J. S. Schaeffer. 2008. Deepwater demersal fish community collapse in Lake Huron. Transactions of the American Fisheries Society 137:1879–1890.

Ruberg, S.A., D.F. Coleman, T.H. Johengen, G.A. Meadows, H.W. Sumeren, G.A. Lang, B.A. Biddanda. 2005. Groundwater plume mapping in a submerged sinkhole in Lake Huron. Marine Technology Society Journal 39(2):65-69.

Schertzer, W.M., R.A. Assel, D. Beletsky, T.E. Croley II, B.M. Lofgren, J.H. Saylor and D. Schwab. 2008. Lake Huron climatology, inter-lake exchange and mean circulation. Aquatic Ecosystem Health & Management 11(2):144-152.

Sellinger, C.E., C.A. Stow, E.C. Lamon, S.S. Qian. 2008. Recent water level declines in the Lake Michigan-Huron system. Environ. Sci. Technol. 42:367–373.

Tanner, H.H. 1987. Atlas of Great Lakes Indian history. University of Oklahoma Press, *Norman*, Okla.

TBNMS (Thunder Bay National Marine Sanctuary). 2009. Thunder Bay National Marine Sanctuary: Final Management Plan. 43pp. Electronic document available from: http://thunderbay.noaa.gov/management/mpr/welcome.html

The Alpena News. July 16, 1971: 3, col. 2.

U.S. Comptroller General. 1977. U.S. Great Lakes Commercial Fishing Industry—Past, Present, and Potential. Washington, D.C. 98 pp.

USEPA (Environmental Protection Agency) and Environment Canada. 1988. The Great Lakes: an environmental atlas and resource book. USEPA, Chicago, and Environment Canada, Toronto, Ontario.

USEPA (Environmental Protection Agency) and Environment Canada. 2009. State of the Great Lakes 2009. 16pp. Electronic document available from: http://binational.net/solec/sogl2009/sogl_2009_h_en.pdf

USFWS (U.S. Fish and Wildlife Service). 1988. Final fish and wildlife coordination act report on biological resources impacted by the proposed navigation season extension to January 31 on the upper Great Lakes. East Lansing Michigan Enhancement Field Office.

USFWS and U.S. Dept. of Commerce Census Bureau. 2007. 2006 National survey of fishing, hunting and wildlife associated recreation.

Vanderploeg, H.A., T.F. Nalepa, D.J. Jude, E.L. Mills, K.T. Holbeck, J.R. Liebig, I.A. Grigorovich, H. Ojaveer. 2002. Dispersal and emerging ecological impacts of Ponto-Caspian species in the Laurentian Great Lakes. Canadian Journal of Fisheries and Aquatic Sciences 59:1209-1228.

Voorhies, A.A., B.A. Biddanda, S.T. Kendall, S. Jain, D.N. Marcus, S.C. Nold, N.D. Sheldon, G.J. Dick. 2012. Cyanobacterial life at low O_2: community genomics and function reveal metabolic versatility and extremely low diversity in a Great Lakes sinkhole mat. Geobiology 10(3):250-267.

Wagner, D., E. Mielbrecht, R. van Woesik. 2008. Application of landscape ecology to spatio-temporal variance of water-quality parameters along the Florida Keys reef tract. Bull Marine Science 83(3):553-569.

Wang, Jia, B. Xuezhi, H. Haoguo, A. Clites, M. Colton, B. Lofgren. 2012. Temporal and spatial variability of Great Lakes ice cover, 1973–2010. J. Climate 25:1318–1329.

Warner, T.D. and D.F. Holecek. 1975. The Thunder Bay shipwreck survey study report. Recreation Research and Planning Unit, Department of Park and Recreation Resources, Michigan State University, East Lansing.

Watzin, M.C., A.B. Cohn, B.P. Emerson. 2001. Zebra mussels, shipwrecks, and the environment, final report. University of Vermont, School of Natural Resources. 55pp. Electronic document available from: www.history.navy.mil/branches/UA_ZebraMussels.pdf

Wetzel, R.G. 1983. Limnology. Saunders College Publishing, New York.

Additional Resources[18]

Alpena County George N. Fletcher Public Library: http://www.alpenalibrary.org

Great Lakes Commission: http://www.glc.org

Great Ships Initiative: http://www.nemw.org/GSI

Habitattiude: http://www.habitattitude.net

Michigan Historical Center: http://www.michigan.gov/michiganhistory

National Oceanic and Atmospheric Administration (NOAA): http://www.noaa.gov

NOAA Climate Database Modernization Program: http://www.ncdc.noaa.gov/oa/climate/cdmp

NOAA Ocean Explorer: http://oceanexplorer.noaa.gov

NOAA Office of Coast Survey: http://www.nauticalcharts.noaa.gov

NOAA Office of National Marine Sanctuaries: http://sanctuaries.noaa.gov

Stop Aquatic Hitchhikers! http://www.protectyourwaters.net

Thunder Bay National Marine Sanctuary: http://thunderbay.noaa.gov

Thunder Bay Sanctuary Research Collection Vessel Database: http://www.greatlakesships.org

U.S. Coast Guard http://www.uscg.mil

University of Wisconsin-Superior's Jim Dan Hill Library: http://www.uwsuper.edu/specialcollections

---

[18] Also see tex box on **page 41** for a list of he sanctuary's research partners.

Appendix A: Rating Scheme for System-Wide Monitoring Questions

The purpose of this appendix is to clarify the 17 questions and possible responses used to report the condition of sanctuary resources in "Condition Reports" for all national marine sanctuaries. Individual staff and partners utilized this guidance, as well as their own informed and detailed understanding of the site to make judgments about the status and trends of sanctuary resources.

The questions derive from the National Marine Sanctuary System's mission, and a system-wide monitoring framework (NMSP 2004) developed to ensure the timely flow of data and information to those responsible for managing and protecting resources in the ocean and coastal zone, and to those that use, depend on and study the ecosystems encompassed by the sanctuaries. They are being used to guide staff and partners at each of the 14 sites in the sanctuary system in the development of this first periodic sanctuary condition report. Evaluations of status and trends may be based on interpretation of quantitative and, when necessary, non-quantitative assessments and observations of scientists, managers and users.

Judging an ecosystem as having "integrity" implies the relative wholeness of ecosystem structure and function, along with the spatial and temporal variability inherent in these characteristics, as determined by the ecosystem's natural evolutionary history. Ecosystem integrity is reflected in the system's ability to produce and maintain adaptive biotic elements. Fluctuations of a system's natural characteristics, including abiotic drivers, biotic composition, complex relationships, and functional processes and redundancies are unaltered and are either likely to persist or be regained following natural disturbance.

Not all questions, however, use ecosystem integrity as a basis for judgment. One focuses on the impacts of water quality factors on human health. Another rates the status of key species compared with that expected in an unaltered ecosystem. One rates maritime archaeological resources based on their historical, archaeological, scientific, and educational value. Another considers the level and persistence of localized threats posed by degrading archaeological resources. Finally, four ask specifically about the levels of on-going human activity that could affect resource condition.

Thunder Bay National Marine Sanctuary regulations specify the management of only cultural resources. Therefore, at present, the sanctuary manages only shipwrecks and related maritime archaeological resources and the public's access to these resources, and not ecological resources. Consequently, this condition report does not directly address other aspects of the ecosystem. Specifically, Questions 5, 6, 7 and 8 relating to Habitat and Questions 9, 10, 12, and 13 relating to Living Resources were deemed not applicable due to the scope of sanctuary management regulations and therefore, responses to these questions have not been provided. Exceptions, however, occur when the natural resource-based questions can be addressed in the context of how that ecosystem element impacts maritime archaeological resources and the public's access to these resources. For this reason, Questions 1, 2, 3, and 4 relating to Water Quality are answered, as are Questions 11 and 14 relating to non-indigenous species. The descriptions that follow each question in this Appendix, which were designed to accommodate all marine sanctuaries, are focused primarily on impacts to the ecosystem integrity of the system. Exceptions have been noted when, for the purposes of this report, different criteria related to maritime archaeological resources and the public's access to these resources were used to judge status and trends.

Following a brief discussion about each question, statements are presented that were used to judge the status and assign a corresponding color code. These statements are customized for each question. In addition, the following options are available for all questions: " N/A" - the question does not apply; and "Undet." - resource status is undetermined.

Symbols used to indicate trends are the same for all questions: "▲" - conditions appear to be improving; "▬" - conditions do not appear to be changing; "▼" - conditions appear to be declining; and "?" – trend is undetermined.

Water Stressors

1. | **Are specific or multiple stressors, including changing oceanographic and atmospheric conditions, affecting water quality and how are they changing?**

This is meant to capture shifts in condition arising from certain changing physical processes and anthropogenic inputs. Factors resulting in regionally accelerated rates of change in water temperature, salinity, dissolved oxygen, or water clarity, could all be judged to reduce water quality. Localized changes in circulation or sedimentation resulting, for example, from coastal construction or dredge spoil disposal, can affect light penetration, salinity regimes, oxygen levels, productivity, waste transport, and other factors that influence habitat, living resource, or maritime archaeological resource quality. Human inputs, generally in the form of contaminants from point or non-point sources, including fertilizers, pesticides, hydrocarbons, heavy metals, and sewage, are common causes of environmental degradation, often in combination rather than alone. Certain biotoxins, such as domoic acid, may be of particular interest to specific sanctuaries.

[Note: For the purposes of the Thunder Bay National Marine Sanctuary Condition Report this question was considered in the context of how stressors to water quality may impact maritime archaeological resource quality and the public's access of these resources.]

Good	Conditions do not appear to have the potential to negatively affect maritime archaeological resources.
Good/Fair	Selected conditions may degrade maritime archaeological resources, but are not likely to cause substantial or persistent declines.
Fair	Selected conditions may cause measurable but not severe declines in maritime archaeological resources.
Fair/Poor	Selected conditions have caused or are likely to cause severe declines in some but not all maritime archaeological resources.
Poor	Selected conditions have caused or are likely to cause severe declines in most if not all maritime archaeological resources.

Water Eutrophic Condition

2. | **What is the eutrophic condition of sanctuary waters and how is it changing?**

Nutrient enrichment often leads to planktonic and/or benthic algae blooms. Some affect benthic communities directly through space competition. Overgrowth and other competitive interactions (e.g., accumulation of algal-sediment mats) often lead to shifts in dominance in the benthic assemblage. Disease incidence and frequency can also be affected by algae competition and the resulting chemistry along competitive boundaries. Blooms can also affect water column conditions, including light penetration and plankton availability, which can alter pelagic food webs, benthic development, and the quality of visitor experiences (e.g., water clarity for divers). Harmful algal blooms often affect resources, as biotoxins are released into the water and air, and oxygen can be depleted.

[Note: For the purposes of the Thunder Bay National Marine Sanctuary Condition Report this question was considered in the context of how eutrophication may impact maritime archaeological resource quality and the public's access of these resources.]

Good	Conditions do not appear to have the potential to negatively affect maritime archaeological resources.
Good/Fair	Selected conditions may degrade maritime archaeological resource quality, but are not likely to cause substantial or persistent declines.
Fair	Selected conditions may cause measurable but not severe declines in maritime archaeological resources.
Fair/Poor	Selected conditions have caused or are likely to cause severe declines in some but not all maritime archaeological resources.
Poor	Selected conditions have caused or are likely to cause severe declines in most if not all maritime archaeological resources.

Water
Human Health

3. | **Do sanctuary waters pose risks to human health and how are they changing?**

Human health concerns are generally raised by evidence of contamination (usually bacterial or chemical) in bathing waters or fish intended for consumption. They also emerge when harmful algal blooms are reported or when cases of respiratory distress or other disorders attributable to harmful algal blooms increase dramatically. Any of these conditions should be considered in the course of judging the risk to humans posed by waters in a marine sanctuary.

Some sites may have access to specific information on beach and shellfish conditions. In particular, beaches may be closed when criteria for safe water body contact are exceeded, or shellfish harvesting may be prohibited when contaminant loads or infection rates exceed certain levels. These conditions can be evaluated in the context of the descriptions below.

[Note: For the purposes of the Thunder Bay National Marine Sanctuary Condition Report this question was considered in the context of how water quality may impact to human health and thus the public's access to maritime archaeological resources.]

Good	Conditions do not appear to have the potential to negatively affect human health.
Good/Fair	Selected conditions that have the potential to affect human health may exist, but human impacts have not been reported.
Fair	Selected conditions have resulted in isolated human impacts, but evidence does not justify widespread or persistent concern.
Fair/Poor	Selected conditions have caused or are likely to cause severe impacts, but cases to date have not suggested a pervasive problem.
Poor	Selected conditions warrant widespread concern and action, as large-scale, persistent and/or repeated severe impacts are likely or have occurred.

Water
Human Activities

4. | **What are the levels of human activities that may influence water quality and how are they changing?**

Among the human activities in or near sanctuaries that affect water quality are those involving direct discharges (transiting vessels, visiting vessels, onshore and offshore industrial facilities, public wastewater facilities), those that contribute contaminants to stream, river, and water control discharges (agriculture, runoff from impermeable surfaces through storm drains, conversion of land use), and those releasing airborne chemicals that subsequently deposit via particulates at sea (vessels, land-based traffic, power plants, manufacturing facilities, refineries). In addition, dredging and trawling can cause resuspension of contaminants in sediments.

[Note: For the purposes of the Thunder Bay National Marine Sanctuary Condition Report this question was considered in the context of how human activities that influence water quality may impact maritime archaeological resources and the public's access of these resources.]

Good	Few or no activities occur that are likely to negatively affect water quality.
Good/Fair	Some potentially harmful activities exist, but they do not appear to have had a negative effect on water quality.
Fair	Selected activities have resulted in measurable resource impacts, but evidence suggests effects are localized, not widespread.
Fair/Poor	Selected activities have caused or are likely to cause severe impacts, and cases to date suggest a pervasive problem.
Poor	Selected activities warrant widespread concern and action, as large-scale, persistent, and/or repeated severe impacts have occurred or are likely to occur.

Habitat Abundance & Distribution

5. What are the abundance and distribution of major habitat types and how are they changing?

Habitat loss is of paramount concern when it comes to protecting marine and terrestrial ecosystems. Of greatest concern to sanctuaries are changes caused, either directly or indirectly, by human activities. The loss of shoreline is recognized as a problem indirectly caused by human activities. Habitats with submerged aquatic vegetation are often altered by changes in water conditions in estuaries, bays and nearshore waters. Intertidal zones can be affected for long periods by spills or by chronic pollutant exposure. Beaches and haul-out areas can be littered with dangerous marine debris, as can the water column or benthic habitats. Sandy subtidal and hard-bottom areas are frequently disturbed or destroyed by trawling. Even rocky areas several hundred meters deep are increasingly affected by certain types of trawls, bottom longlines and fish traps. Groundings, anchors and divers damage submerged reefs. Cables and pipelines disturb corridors across numerous habitat types and can be destructive if they become mobile. Shellfish dredging removes, alters and fragments habitats.

The result of these activities is the gradual reduction of the extent and quality of marine habitats. Losses can often be quantified through visual surveys and to some extent using high-resolution mapping. This question asks about the quality of habitats compared to those that would be expected without human impacts. The status depends on comparison to a baseline that existed in the past, one toward which restoration efforts might aim.

Good	Habitats are in pristine or near-pristine condition and are unlikely to preclude full community development.
Good/Fair	Selected habitat loss or alteration has taken place, precluding full development of living resource assemblages, but it is unlikely to cause substantial or persistent degradation in living resources or water quality.
Fair	Selected habitat loss or alteration may inhibit the development of assemblages, and may cause measurable but not severe declines in living resources or water quality.
Fair/Poor	Selected habitat loss or alteration has caused or is likely to cause severe declines in some but not all living resources or water quality.
Poor	Selected habitat loss or alteration has caused or is likely to cause severe declines in most if not all living resources or water quality.

Habitat Structure

6. | **What is the condition of biologically structured habitats and how is it changing?**

Many organisms depend on the integrity of their habitats and that integrity is largely determined by the condition of particular living organisms. Coral reefs may be the best known examples of such biologically structured habitats. Not only is the substrate itself biogenic, but the diverse assemblages residing within and on the reefs depend on and interact with each other in tightly linked food webs. They also depend on each other for the recycling of wastes, hygiene, and the maintenance of water quality, among other requirements.

Kelp beds may not be biogenic habitats to the extent of coral reefs, but kelp provides essential habitat for assemblages that would not reside or function together without it. There are other communities of organisms that are also similarly co-dependent, such as hard-bottom communities, which may be structured by bivalves, octocorals, coralline algae, or other groups that generate essential habitat for other species. Intertidal assemblages structured by mussels, barnacles and algae are another example, seagrass beds another. This question is intended to address these types of places, where organisms form structures (habitats) on which other organisms depend.

Good	Habitats are in pristine or near-pristine condition and are unlikely to preclude full community development.
Good/Fair	Selected habitat loss or alteration has taken place, precluding full development of living resources, but it is unlikely to cause substantial or persistent degradation in living resources or water quality.
Fair	Selected habitat loss or alteration may inhibit the development of living resources, and may cause measurable but not severe declines in living resources or water quality.
Fair/Poor	Selected habitat loss or alteration has caused or is likely to cause severe declines in some but not all living resources or water quality.
Poor	Selected habitat loss or alteration has caused or is likely to cause severe declines in most if not all living resources or water quality.

Habitat Contaminants

7. | **What are the contaminant concentrations in sanctuary habitats and how are they changing?**

This question addresses the need to understand the risk posed by contaminants within benthic formations, such as soft sediments, hard bottoms, or biogenic organisms. In the first two cases, the contaminants can become available when released via disturbance. They can also pass upwards through the food chain after being ingested by bottom dwelling prey species. The contaminants of concern generally include pesticides, hydrocarbons, and heavy metals, but the specific concerns of individual sanctuaries may differ substantially.

Good	Contaminants do not appear to have the potential to negatively affect living resources or water quality.
Good/Fair	Selected contaminants may preclude full development of living resource assemblages, but are not likely to cause substantial or persistent degradation.
Fair	Selected contaminants may inhibit the development of assemblages, and may cause measurable but not severe declines in living resources or water quality.
Fair/Poor	Selected contaminants have caused or are likely to cause severe declines in some but not all living resources or water quality.
Poor	Selected contaminants have caused or are likely to cause severe declines in most if not all living resources or water quality.

Habitat
Human Activities

8. | **What are the levels of human activities that may influence habitat quality and how are they changing?**

Human activities that degrade habitat quality do so by affecting structural (geological), biological, oceanographic, acoustic or chemical characteristics. Structural impacts include removal or mechanical alteration, including various fishing techniques (trawls, traps, dredges, longlines, and even hook-and-line in some habitats), dredging channels and harbors and dumping spoil, vessel groundings, anchoring, laying pipelines and cables, installing offshore structures, discharging drill cuttings, dragging tow cables, and placing artificial reefs. Removal or alteration of critical biological components of habitats can occur along with several of the above activities, most notably trawling, groundings and cable drags.

Marine debris, particularly in large quantities (e.g., lost gill nets and other types of fishing gear), can affect both biological and structural habitat components. Changes in water circulation often occur when channels are dredged, fill is added, coastal areas are reinforced, or other construction takes place. These activities affect habitat by changing food delivery, waste removal, water quality (e.g., salinity, clarity and sedimentation), recruitment patterns, and a host of other factors. Acoustic impacts can occur to water column habitats and organisms from acute and chronic sources of anthropogenic noise (e.g., shipping, boating, construction). Chemical alterations most commonly occur following spills and can have both acute and chronic impacts.

Good — Few or no activities occur that are likely to negatively affect habitat quality.

Good/Fair — Some potentially harmful activities exist, but they do not appear to have had a negative effect on habitat quality.

Fair — Selected activities have resulted in measurable habitat impacts, but evidence suggests effects are localized, not widespread.

Fair/Poor — Selected activities have caused or are likely to cause severe impacts, and cases to date suggest a pervasive problem.

Poor — Selected activities warrant widespread concern and action, as large-scale, persistent and/or repeated severe impacts have occurred or are likely to occur.

Living Resources
Biodiversity

9. | **What is the status of biodiversity and how is it changing?**

This is intended to elicit thought and assessment of the condition of living resources based on expected biodiversity levels and the interactions between species. Intact ecosystems require that all parts not only exist, but that they function together, resulting in natural symbioses, competition, and predator-prey relationships. Community integrity, resistance and resilience all depend on these relationships. Abundance, relative abundance, trophic structure, richness, H' diversity, evenness, and other measures are often used to assess these attributes.

Good — Biodiversity appears to reflect pristine or near-pristine conditions and promotes ecosystem integrity (full community development and function).

Good/Fair — Selected biodiversity loss has taken place, precluding full community development and function, but it is unlikely to cause substantial or persistent degradation of ecosystem integrity.

Fair — Selected biodiversity loss may inhibit full community development and function, and may cause measurable but not severe degradation of ecosystem integrity.

Fair/Poor — Selected biodiversity loss has caused or is likely to cause severe declines in some but not all ecosystem components and reduce ecosystem integrity.

Poor — Selected biodiversity loss has caused or is likely to cause severe declines in ecosystem integrity.

Living Resources
Extracted Species

10. | **What is the status of environmentally sustainable fishing and how is it changing?**

Commercial and recreational harvesting are highly selective activities, for which fishers and collectors target a limited number of species, and often remove high proportions of populations. In addition to removing significant amounts of biomass from the ecosystem, reducing its availability to other consumers, these activities tend to disrupt specific and often critical food web links. When too much extraction occurs (i.e. ecologically unsustainable harvesting), trophic cascades ensue, resulting in changes in the abundance of non-targeted species as well. It also reduces the ability of the targeted species to replenish populations at a rate that supports continued ecosystem integrity.

It is essential to understand whether removals are occurring at ecologically sustainable levels. Knowing extraction levels and determining the impacts of removal are both ways that help gain this understanding. Measures for target species of abundance, catch amounts or rates (e.g., catch per unit effort), trophic structure, and changes in non-target species abundance are all generally used to assess these conditions.

Other issues related to this question include whether fishers are using gear that is compatible with the habitats being fished and whether that gear minimizes by-catch and incidental take of marine mammals. For example, bottom-tending gear often destroys or alters both benthic structure and non-targeted animal and plant communities. "Ghost fishing" occurs when lost traps continue to capture organisms. Lost or active nets, as well as lines used to mark and tend traps and other fishing gear, can entangle marine mammals. Any of these could be considered indications of environmentally unsustainable fishing techniques.

■	Good	Extraction does not appear to affect ecosystem integrity (full community development and function).
■	Good/Fair	Extraction takes place, precluding full community development and function, but it is unlikely to cause substantial or persistent degradation of ecosystem integrity.
■	Fair	Extraction may inhibit full community development and function, and may cause measurable but not severe degradation of ecosystem integrity.
■	Fair/Poor	Extraction has caused or is likely to cause severe declines in some but not all ecosystem components and reduce ecosystem integrity.
■	Poor	Extraction has caused or is likely to cause severe declines in ecosystem integrity.

Living Resources
Non-Indigenous Species

11. | **What is the status of non-indigenous species and how is it changing?**

Non-indigenous species are generally considered problematic, and candidates for rapid response, if found, soon after invasion. For those that become established, their impacts can sometimes be assessed by quantifying changes in the affected native species. This question allows sanctuaries to report on the threat posed by non-indigenous species. In some cases, the presence of a species alone constitutes a significant threat (certain invasive algae). In other cases, impacts have been measured, and may or may not significantly affect ecosystem integrity or maritime archaeological resource quality.

[Note: For the purposes of the Thunder Bay National Marine Sanctuary Condition Report this question was considered in the context of how non-indigenous species may impact maritime archaeological resource quality and the public's access of these resources.]

■	Good	Non-indigenous species are not suspected or do not appear to affect maritime archaeological resources.
■	Good/Fair	Non-indigenous species exist, but are unlikely to cause substantial or persistent degradation of archaeological resources.
■	Fair	Non-indigenous species may cause measurable but not severe degradation of maritime archaeological resources.
■	Fair/Poor	Non-indigenous species have caused or are likely to cause severe declines in some but not all maritime archaeological resources.
■	Poor	Non-indigenous species have caused or are likely to cause severe declines in maritime archaeological resources.

Living Resources
Key Species

12. | **What is the status of key species and how is it changing?**

Certain species can be defined as "key" within a marine sanctuary. Some might be keystone species, that is, species on which the persistence of a large number of other species in the ecosystem depends — pillars of community stability. Their functional contribution to ecosystem function is disproportionate to their numerical abundance or biomass, and their impact is therefore important at the community or ecosystem level. Their removal initiates changes in ecosystem structure and sometimes the disappearance of or dramatic increase in the abundance of dependent species. Keystone species may include certain habitat modifiers, predators, herbivores and organisms involved in critical symbiotic relationships (e.g., cleaning or co-habitating species).

Other key species may include those that are indicators of ecosystem condition or change (e.g., particularly sensitive species), those targeted for special protection efforts, or charismatic species that are identified with certain areas or ecosystems. These may or may not meet the definition of keystone, but do require assessments of status and trends.

Good	Key and keystone species appear to reflect pristine or near-pristine conditions and may promote ecosystem integrity (full community development and function).
Good/Fair	Selected key or keystone species are at reduced levels, perhaps precluding full community development and function, but substantial or persistent declines are not expected.
Fair	The reduced abundance of selected keystone species may inhibit full community development and function, and may cause measurable but not severe degradation of ecosystem integrity; or selected key species are at reduced levels, but recovery is possible.
Fair/Poor	The reduced abundance of selected keystone species has caused or is likely to cause severe declines in some but not all ecosystem components, and reduce ecosystem integrity; or selected key species are at substantially reduced levels, and prospects for recovery are uncertain.
Poor	The reduced abundance of selected keystone species has caused or is likely to cause severe declines in ecosystem integrity; or selected key species are at severely reduced levels, and recovery is unlikely.

Living Resources
Health of Key
Species

13. | **What is the condition or health of key species and how is it changing?**

For those species considered essential to ecosystem integrity, measures of their condition can be important to determining the likelihood that they will persist and continue to provide vital ecosystem functions. Measures of condition may include growth rates, fecundity, recruitment, age-specific survival, tissue contaminant levels, pathologies (disease incidence tumors, deformities), the presence and abundance of critical symbionts, or parasite loads. Similar measures of condition may also be appropriate for other key species (indicator, protected, or charismatic species). In contrast to the question about keystone species (#12 above), the impact of changes in the abundance or condition of key species is more likely to be observed at the population or individual level, and less likely to result in ecosystem or community effects.

Good	The condition of key resources appears to reflect pristine or near-pristine conditions.
Good/Fair	The condition of selected key resources is not optimal, perhaps precluding full ecological function, but substantial or persistent declines are not expected.
Fair	The diminished condition of selected key resources may cause a measurable but not severe reduction in ecological function, but recovery is possible.
Fair/Poor	The comparatively poor condition of selected key resources makes prospects for recovery uncertain.
Poor	The poor condition of selected key resources makes recovery unlikely.

Living Resources
Human Activities

14. | **What are the levels of human activities that may influence living resource quality and how are they changing?**

Human activities that degrade living resource quality do so by causing a loss or reduction of one or more species, by disrupting critical life stages, by impairing various physiological processes, or by promoting the introduction of non-indigenous species or pathogens. (Note: Activities that impact habitat and water quality may also affect living resources. These activities are dealt with in Questions 4 and 8, and many are repeated here as they also have direct effect on living resources).

Fishing and collecting are the primary means of removing resources. Bottom trawling, seine-fishing, and the collection of ornamental species for the aquarium trade are all common examples, some being more selective than others. Chronic mortality can be caused by marine debris derived from commercial or recreational vessel traffic, lost fishing gear, and excess visitation, resulting in the gradual loss of some species.

Critical life stages can be affected in various ways. Mortality to adult stages is often caused by trawling and other fishing techniques, cable drags, dumping spoil or drill cuttings, vessel groundings, or persistent anchoring. Contamination of areas by acute or chronic spills, discharges by vessels, or municipal and industrial facilities can make them unsuitable for recruitment; the same activities can make nursery habitats unsuitable. Although coastal armoring and construction can increase the availability of surfaces suitable for the recruitment and growth of hard-bottom species, the activity may disrupt recruitment patterns for other species (e.g., intertidal soft-bottom animals) and habitat may be lost.

Spills, discharges and contaminants released from sediments (e.g., by dredging and dumping) can all cause physiological impairment and tissue contamination. Such activities can affect all life stages by reducing fecundity, increasing larval, juvenile, and adult mortality, reducing disease resistance, and increasing susceptibility to predation. Bioaccumulation allows some contaminants to move upward through the food chain, disproportionately affecting certain species.

Activities that promote introductions include bilge discharges and ballast water exchange, commercial shipping and vessel transportation. Releases of aquarium fish can also lead to species introductions.

[Note: For the purposes of the Thunder Bay National Marine Sanctuary Condition Report this question was considered in the context of how human activities that influence living resources may impact maritime archaeological resources and the public's access of these resources.]

	Good	Few or no activities occur that are likely to negatively affect maritime archaeological resources.
	Good/Fair	Some potentially harmful activities exist, but they do not appear to have had a negative effect on maritime archaeological resources.
	Fair	Selected activities have resulted in measurable impacts to maritime archaeological resources, but evidence suggests effects are localized, not widespread.
	Fair/Poor	Selected activities have caused or are likely to cause severe impacts to maritime archaeological resources, and cases to date suggest a pervasive problem.
	Poor	Selected activities warrant widespread concern and action, as large-scale, persistent, and/or repeated severe impacts to maritime archaeological resources have occurred or are likely to occur.

Maritime Archaeological Resources
Integrity

15. | **What is the integrity of known maritime archaeological resources and how is it changing?**

The condition of archaeological resources in a marine sanctuary significantly affects their value for science and education, as well as the resource's eligibility for listing in the National Register of Historic Places. Assessments of archaeological sites include evaluation of the apparent levels of site integrity, which are based on levels of previous human disturbance and the level of natural deterioration. The historical, scientific and educational values of sites are also evaluated, and are substantially determined and affected by site condition.

Good	Known archaeological resources appear to reflect little or no unexpected disturbance.
Good/Fair	Selected archaeological resources exhibit indications of disturbance, but there appears to have been little or no reduction in historical, scientific, or educational value.
Fair	The diminished condition of selected archaeological resources has reduced, to some extent, their historical, scientific, or educational value, and may affect the eligibility of some sites for listing in the National Register of Historic Places.
Fair/Poor	The diminished condition of selected archaeological resources has substantially reduced their historical, scientific, or educational value, and is likely to affect their eligibility for listing in the National Register of Historic Places.
Poor	The degraded condition of known archaeological resources in general makes them ineffective in terms of historical, scientific, or educational value, and precludes their listing in the National Register of Historic Places.

Maritime Archaeological Resources
Threat to Environment

16. | **Do known maritime archaeological resources pose an environmental hazard and how is this threat changing?**

The sinking of a ship potentially introduces hazardous materials into the marine environment. This danger is true for historic shipwrecks as well. The issue is complicated by the fact that shipwrecks older than 50 years may be considered historical resources and must, by federal mandate, be protected. Many historic shipwrecks, particularly early to mid-20th century, still have the potential to retain oil and fuel in tanks and bunkers. As shipwrecks age and deteriorate, the potential for release of these materials into the environment increases.

Good	Known maritime archaeological resources pose few or no environmental threats.
Good/Fair	Selected maritime archaeological resources may pose isolated or limited environmental threats, but substantial or persistent impacts are not expected.
Fair	Selected maritime archaeological resources may cause measurable, but not severe, impacts to certain sanctuary resources or areas, but recovery is possible.
Fair/Poor	Selected maritime archaeological resources pose substantial threats to certain sanctuary resources or areas, and prospects for recovery are uncertain.
Poor	Selected maritime archaeological resources pose serious threats to sanctuary resources, and recovery is unlikely.

Maritime Archaeological Resources
Human Activities

17. | **What are the levels of human activities that may influence maritime archaeological resource quality and how are they changing?**

Some human maritime activities threaten the physical integrity of submerged archaeological resources. Archaeological site integrity is compromised when elements are moved, removed, or otherwise damaged. Threats come from looting by divers, inadvertent damage by scuba diving visitors, improperly conducted archaeology that does not fully document site disturbance, anchoring, groundings, and commercial and recreational fishing activities, among others.

Good — Few or no activities occur that are likely to negatively affect maritime archaeological resource integrity.

Good/Fair — Some potentially relevant activities exist, but they do not appear to have had a negative effect on maritime archaeological resource integrity.

Fair — Selected activities have resulted in measurable impacts to maritime archaeological resources, but evidence suggests effects are localized, not widespread.

Fair/Poor — Selected activities have caused or are likely to cause severe impacts, and cases to date suggest a pervasive problem.

Poor — Selected activities warrant widespread concern and action, as large-scale, persistent, and/or repeated severe impacts have occurred or are likely to occur.

Appendix B: Consultation with Experts and Document Review

The process for preparing condition reports involves a combination of accepted techniques for collecting and interpreting information gathered from subject matter experts. The approach varies somewhat from sanctuary to sanctuary, in order to accommodate differing styles for working with partners. The Thunder Bay National Marine Sanctuary approach was closely related to the Delphi Method, a technique designed to organize group communication among a panel of geographically dispersed experts by using questionnaires, ultimately facilitating the formation of a group judgment. This method can be applied when it is necessary for decision-makers to combine the testimony of a group of experts, whether in the form of facts or informed opinion, or both, into a single useful statement.

The Delphi Method relies on repeated interactions with experts who respond to questions with a limited number of choices to arrive at the best supported answers. Feedback to the experts allows them to refine their views, gradually moving the group toward the most agreeable judgment. For condition reports, the Office of National Marine Sanctuaries uses 17 questions related to the status and trends of sanctuary resources, with accompanying descriptions and five possible choices that describe resource conditions (Appendix A).

In order to address the 17 questions, sanctuary staff selected and consulted outside experts familiar with water quality, living resources, habitat, and maritime archaeological resources. A small workshop was convened in March 2010 where experts from NOAA Great Lakes Environmental Research Laboratory (GLERL) participated in facilitated discussions about each of the 17 questions. At the workshop each expert was introduced to the questions, was then asked to provide recommendations and supporting arguments and the group supplemented the input with further discussion. In order to ensure consistency with Delphic methods, a critical role of the facilitator was to minimize dominance of the discussion by a single individual or opinion (which often leads to "follow the leader" tendencies in group meetings) and to encourage the expression of honest differences of opinion. As discussions progressed, the group converged in their opinion of the rating that most accurately describes the current resource condition. After an appropriate amount of time, the facilitator asked whether the group could agree on a rating for the question, as defined by specific language linked to each rating (see Appendix A). If an agreement was reached, the result was recorded and the group moved on to consider the trend in the same manner. If agreement was not reached, the facilitator instructed sanctuary staff to consider all input and decide on a rating and trend at a future time, and to send their ratings back to workshop participants for individual comment.

Experts at the workshops were also given the opportunity to qualify their level of confidence in status and trend ratings by characterizing the sources of information they used to make judgments. A ranking of information quality was provided for three potential categories: data, literature, and personal experience. For each status or trend rating, the experts documented the source of information for each category.

LEVEL OF CONFIDENCE				
1	2	3	4	5
High Uncertainty	Speculative	Reasonable Inference	Moderate Certainty	High Certainty
No data are available, and no substantive personal experience	Few data and little information available, and limited personal experience	Some data available, unpublished or in non-peer reviewed sources, or some direct personal experience.	Data available, some peer-reviewed publications exist, or direct personal experience	Considerable data available, extensive record of publication, or extensive personal experience or expertise

The scores compiled during the workshop were as follows:

QUESTION	DATA	LITERATURE	PERSONAL EXPERIENCE
1	2	2	3
2	3	3	3
3	3	1	1
4	3	1	1
5	N/A	N/A	N/A
6	N/A	N/A	N/A
7	N/A	N/A	N/A
8	N/A	N/A	N/A
9	N/A	N/A	N/A
10	N/A	N/A	N/A
11	4	4	4
12	N/A	N/A	N/A
13	N/A	N/A	N/A
14	3	3	3
15	3	2	3
16	3	2	3
17	2	1	3

The first draft of the document summarized the opinions and uncertainty expressed by the experts, who based their input on knowledge and perceptions of local conditions. Comments and citations received from the experts were included, as appropriate, in text supporting the ratings.

The first draft of the document was sent to the subject experts from GLERL who attended the workshop for what was called an initial review — a four-week period that allows experts to ensure that the report accurately reflected their input, identify information gaps, provide comments, or suggest revisions to the ratings and text. During this four-week period, the report was also distributed to representatives from the NOAA National Marine Fisheries Service, NOAA Office of National Marine Sanctuaries, NOAA Marine Debris Program, and Michigan Department of Natural Resources. These individuals were asked to review the technical merits of resource ratings and accompanying text, as well as to point out any omissions or factual errors. Upon receiving reviewer comments, the writing team revised the text and ratings as they deemed appropriate.

A draft final report was then sent for external peer review, a requirement that started in December 2004, when the White House Office of Management and Budget (OMB) issued a Final Information Quality Bulletin for Peer Review (OMB Bulletin) establishing peer review standards that would enhance the quality and credibility of the federal government's scientific information. Along with other information, these standards apply to Influential Scientific Information, which is information that can reasonably be determined to have a "clear and substantial impact on important public policies or private sector decisions." The condition reports are considered Influential Scientific Information. For this reason, these reports are subject to the review requirements of both the Information Quality Act and the OMB Bulletin guidelines. Therefore, following the completion of every condition report, they are reviewed by a minimum of three individuals who are considered to be experts in their field, were not involved in the development of the report, and are not ONMS employees. Comments from these peer reviews were incorporated into the final text of the report. Furthermore, OMB Bulletin guidelines require that reviewer comments, names, and affiliations be posted on the agency website:

http://www.osec.doc.gov/cio/oipr/pr_plans.htm. Reviewer comments, however, are not attributed to specific individuals. Comments by the external peer reviewers are posted at the same time as the formatted final document.

Following the external peer review, the comments and recommendations of the reviewers were considered by sanctuary staff and incorporated, as appropriate, into a final draft document. In some cases, sanctuary staff reevaluated the status and trend ratings and when appropriate, the accompanying text in the document was edited to reflect the new ratings. The final interpretation, ratings and text in the draft condition report were the responsibility of sanctuary staff, with final approval by the sanctuary manager. To emphasize this important point, authorship of the report is attributed to the sanctuary alone. Subject experts were not authors, though their efforts and affiliations are acknowledged in the report.

Appendix C: List of Known Shipwrecks in the Thunder Bay Region

Known Shipwrecks within the Thunder Bay National Marine Sanctuary									
VESSEL NAME	VESSEL TYPE	HULL	BUILT	LOST	LENGTH	LOSS TYPE	CARGO	COUNTY	DEPTH
Allen, E.B.	Schooner	Wood	1864	1871	134	Collision	Grain	Alpena	100
Barge No. 012	Barge	Steel	1897	1975	160	Collision	Supplies	Alpena	40
Barge No. 083	Barge	Wood	1920	1941	200	Foundered	Well-drilling Machinery	Alpena	70
Bay City	Schooner Barge	Wood	1857	1902	146	Collision	Light	Alpena	11
Bissell, Harvey	Schooner	Wood	1866	1905	162	Abandoned	Lumber	Alpena	15
Blanchard, B.W.	Steam Barge	Wood	1870	1904	221	Stranded	Lumber	Alpena	9
Congress	Propeller	Wood	1861	1868	139	Stranded, Burned	Salt, Apples, Rail Iron	Alpena	17
Corsican	Schooner	Wood	1862	1893	112	Collision	Coal	Alpena	160
Davidson, James	Bulk Freighter	Wood	1874	1883	230	Stranded	Coal	Alpena	38
Deck Barge	Barge	Steel	Unknown	Unknown	60	Foundered	Unknown	Alpena	92
Empire State	Brigantine	Wood	1862	1877	136	Stranded	Iron Ore	Alpena	12
Flint, Oscar T.	Steam Barge	Wood	1889	1909	218	Burned	Limestone	Alpena	32
Franklin, Benjamin	Paddle Wheeler	Wood	1842	1850	135	Stranded	Light	Alpena	15
Galena	Steam Barge	Wood	1857	1872	190	Stranded	Lumber	Alpena	16
Grecian	Bulk Freighter	Steel	1891	1906	296	Foundered	Light	Alpena	98
Hall, James H.	Schooner	Wood	1885	1916	91	Stranded	Lumber	Alpena	6
Haltiner's Barge	Dredge	Wood	Unknown	1927	80	Foundered	Dredging Equipment	Alpena	17
Hanna, D.R.	Bulk Freighter	Steel	1906	1919	532	Collision	Wheat	Alpena	130
Johnson, John T.	Schooner Barge	Wood	1873	1904	171	Stranded	Lumber	Alpena	7
Knight Templar	Schooner Barge	Wood	1865	1903	136	Abandoned	Light	Alpena	5
Lake Michigan Car Ferry Barge No. 1	Barge	Wood	1895	1918	309	Foundered	Lumber, Chickens	Alpena	42
Light Guard	Schooner	Wood	1866	1903	143	Abandoned	Light	Alpena	6
Maid of the Mist	Schooner	Wood	1863	1878	90	Stranded	Cedar Posts	Alpena	7
Maxwell, William	Tug	Wood	1883	1908	66	Stranded	Fish	Alpena	12
Monohansett	Steam Barge	Wood	1872	1907	164	Burned	Coal	Alpena	18
Montana	Steam Barge	Wood	1872	1914	236	Burned	Light	Alpena	66
Murray Company Dredge "Heart Failure"	Dredge	Wood	Unknown	Unknown	Unkown	Abandoned	Light	Alpena	18
New Orleans	Paddle Wheeler	Wood	1838	1849	185	Stranded	Freight	Alpena	13
New Orleans	Bulk Freighter	Wood	1885	1906	231	Collision	Coal	Alpena	130
Nordmeer	Ocean Vessel	Steel	1954	1966	470	Stranded	Steel	Alpena	35
Ogarita	Barkentine	Wood	1864	1905	173	Burned	Coal	Alpena	30
Palmer, E B.	Schooner	Wood	1856	1892	138	Stranded	Red Sandstone	Alpena	16
Parks, O.E.	Steam Barge	Wood	1891	1929	134	Foundered	Pulpwood	Alpena	62
Pewabic	Propeller	Wood	1863	1865	198	Collision	Copper	Alpena	170
Portsmouth	Propeller	Wood	1853	1867	182	Stranded	Pig Iron	Alpena	8

Table is continued on the following page.

Known Shipwrecks within the Thunder Bay National Marine Sanctuary (Continued)

VESSEL NAME	VESSEL TYPE	HULL	BUILT	LOST	LENGTH	LOSS TYPE	CARGO	COUNTY	DEPTH
Rend, W P.	Steam Barge	Wood	1888	1917	287	Stranded	Stone	Alpena	17
Scott, Isaac M.	Bulk Freighter	Steel	1909	1913	524	Foundered	Coal	Alpena	175
Shamrock	Steam Barge	Wood	1875	1905	146	Abandoned	Lumber	Alpena	11
Spud Barge	Barge	Wood	Unknown	1937	Unkown	Abandoned	Unknown	Alpena	1
Stevens, William H.	Schooner	Wood	1855	1863	117	Stranded	Wheat	Alpena	10
Thew, William P.	Steam Barge	Wood	1884	1909	132	Collision	Light	Alpena	84
Van Valkenburg, Lucinda	Schooner	Wood	1862	1887	128	Collision	Coal	Alpena	60
Viator	Ocean Vessel	Steel	1904	1935	231	Collision	Pickled Herring	Alpena	188
Warner, John F.	Schooner, 2 mast	Wood	1855	1890	126	Abandoned	Lumber, Lath	Alpena	9
Wilson, D.M.	Bulk Freighter	Wood	1873	1894	179	Foundered	Coal	Alpena	48

Additional Known Shipwrecks in the Region

VESSEL NAME	VESSEL TYPE	HULL	BUILT	LOST	LENGTH	LOSS TYPE	CARGO	COUNTY	DEPTH
Albany	Paddle Wheeler	Wood	1846	1853	202	Stranded	Provisions	Presque Isle	5
Audubon, John J.	Schooner	Wood	1854	1854	148	Collision	Rail Iron	Presque Isle	170
American Union	Schooner	Wood	1862	1894	185	Stranded	Light	Presque Isle	8
Barney, D N.	Schooner	Wood	1845	1849	110	Stranded	Clay	Presque Isle	5
Barney, F.T.	Schooner	Wood	1856	1868	126	Collision	Coal	Presque Isle	160
Bentley, James R.	schooner	Wood	1867	1878	178	Foundered	Rye	Presque Isle	165
Black River Wreck	Schooner	Wood	Unknown	Unkown	Unkown	Unkown	Unkown	Alcona	6
Buckingham, Alvin	Schooner	Wood	1853	1870	124	Stranded	Iron Ore	Alcona	8
City of Alpena	Tug	Wood	1874	1880	72	Burned	Light	Alcona	9
Corsair	Schooner	Wood	1866	1872	133	Foundered	Iron Ore	Alcona	170
Defiance	Schooner	Wood	1848	1854	115	Collision	Corn, Wheat	Presque Isle	185
Detroit	Paddle Wheeler	Wood	1859	1872	240	Stranded	Unkown	Alcona	15
Dump Scow	Barge	Wood	Unknown	1930	Unkown	Foundered	Unkown	Presque Isle	130
Duncan City	Tug	Wood	1883	1923	104	Abandoned	Light	Presque Isle	15
Eddy, Newell A.	Schooner	Wood	1890	1893	242	Foundered	Wheat	Mackinaw	168
Egyptian	Bulk Freighter	Wood	1873	1897	232	Burned	Coal	Alcona	260
Etruria	Bulk Freighter	Steel	1902	1905	414	Collision	Coal	Presque Isle	310
Fay, Joseph S.	Bulk Freighter	Wood	1871	1905	215	Stranded	Iron Ore	Presque Isle	17
Florida	Package Freighter	Wood	1889	1897	270	Collision	Package Freight	Presque Isle	206
Franz, W.C.	Bulk Freighter	Steel	1901	1934	346	Collision	Light	Alcona	230
Gilbert, W H.	Bulk Freighter	Steel	1892	1914	328	Collision	Coal	Alcona	255
Greenbush Wreck	Unkown	Wood	Unkown	Unknown	Unkown	Unkown	Unkown	Alcona	10
Handy, Augustus	Schooner	Wood	1855	1861	126	Stranded	Wheat	Mackinaw	U/A

Table is continued on the following page.

VESSEL NAME	VESSEL TYPE	HULL	BUILT	LOST	LENGTH	LOSS TYPE	CARGO	COUNTY	DEPTH
Additional Known Shipwrecks in the Region (Continued)									
Hayes, Kate	Schooner	Wood	1856	1856	130	Stranded	Wheat	Mackinaw	U/A
Ishpeming	Schooner Barge	Wood	1872	1903	157	Stranded	Coal	Alcona	12
Jewett, John	Schooner	Wood	1866	1898	91	Stranded	Unkown	Presque Isle	10
Johnson, Henry J.	Bulk Freighter	Wood	1888	1902	260	Collision	Iron Ore	Presque Isle	160
Jones, Chester B.	Schooner	Wood	1873	1924	167	Abandoned	Lightz	Presque Isle	16
Loretta	Steam Barge	Wood	1892	1896	140	Burned	Chain	Alcona	7
Marine City	Paddle Wheeler	Wood	1866	1880	192	Burned	Shingles, Fish	Alcona	5
Mason, W.G.	Tug	Wood	1898	1924	84	Abandoned	Light	Presque Isle	13
Merrick, M.F.	Schooner	Wood	1863	1889	137	Collision	Furnace Sand	Presque Isle	300
Messenger	Steam Barge	Wood	1866	1890	136	Burned	Cedar	Presque Isle	194
Monrovia	Ocean Vessel	Steel	1943	1959	447	Collision	Steel	Alpena	140
New York	Package Freighter	Wood	1879	1910	268	Foundered	Freight	Alcona	90
Nightingale	Schooner	Wood	1856	1869	138	Stranded	Iron Ore	Mackinaw	70
Norman	Bulk Freighter	Steel	1890	1895	296	Collision	Light	Presque Isle	200
North Bay Wreck	Schooner	Wood	Unkown	Unkown	Unkown	Unkown	Unkown	Presque Isle	15
Northern Light	Barge	Wood	1858	1880	210	Stranded	Unkown	Alcona	2
Northwestern	Brig	Wood	1847	1850	110	Collision	Salt	Presque Isle	135
Persian	schooner	Wood	1855	1868	115	Collision	Wheat	Presque Isle	172
Portland	Schooner	Wood	1863	1877	150	Stranded	Salt	Presque Isle	6
Shaw, John L.	Schooner	Wood	1885	1894	205	Foundered	Coal	Alcona	118
Smith, Anna	Bulk Freighter	Wood	1873	1889	178	Stranded	Coal	Cheboygan	10
Spangler, Kyle	Brig	Wood	1856	1860	130	Foundered	Corn	Presque Isle	185
Typo	Schooner	Wood	1873	1899	137	Collision	Coal	Presque Isle	155
Windiate, Cornelia B.	Schooner	Wood	1874	1875	136	Foundered	Grain	Presque Isle	190

Notes

www.ingramcontent.com/pod-product-compliance
Lightning Source LLC
Chambersburg PA
CBHW080431290526

45791CB00008BA/2456